The Inner Geek in Football

By Luke Wilkins

Preface

I want to start with a confession. *The Inner Geek* suggests that this book represents some sort of personality characteristic; hidden away from the fear and embarrassment that would no doubt accompany any revealing of the real me, and with the next 90-odd pages acting as a kind of cathartic release of secrets. But for anyone who knows me, they will tell you this is not true. There is no *Inner* element to my geekiness; it is as clear to see as a Frank Lampard shot against Germany. If such a thing existed, I would be an *Outer* geek.

I am the guy that only places a bet once he's checked home and away form, goal differentials, and manager ins and outs. The guy that caveats footballing achievements during a pub debate ("yes Wayne Rooney is England's all-time leading goal-scorer, but his goals-to-game ratio is far inferior to that of Jimmy Greaves"). When I was the manager of a local Sunday-league football team I kept records of every player's appearances, goals, cards, and penalties, and printed them out for the end-of-season awards evening. Even now I have an Excel spreadsheet full of data from the league I play in that would make even Opta proud. Which doesn't sound too bad until you realise that the league is a fantasy football one.

But for many of you fans, the geek-side is *Inner.* It has to be. Brad Pitt and Jonah Hill may have done a great job in showing the sporting world that statistics can be useful, but even they haven't managed to fully convert the fan on the street into a data-driven addict of football numbers. At least not in public.

But it is this inner geek that often arises when we watch a game, read a match report, or chat with friends. The commentator mentioned that the Premier League is the most competitive league in the world...the journalist stated that Leicester City are too big to go down...and Dave is adamant that Jose Mourinho is the best manager in the world...Are all these statements true you ask? Well my outer geek is here to answer your inner geek. This book explores all these questions and more so read ahead and see what real data makes of some of the most commonly held beliefs in the world's most popular sport. Just make sure you're hiding it within a *Men's Health* magazine when you read it.

Introduction

There are 15 chapters to this book. The first 11 are the starting team – the core players (analyses) that have been assembled by the manager (yours truly) with the aim of winning the league title (your approval!). Some of these players may be bigger than others. Some of them may be more technically (statistically) astute than others. And they'll likely all have different strengths and weaknesses. But hopefully these players will combine for a winning formula. And like all good teams, they are backed up by a solid substitute's bench, starting with the End of Season Review. This is the experienced pro who gets brought on to see a game out. Like Paul Scholes in the twilight of his career, it will link everything together and may even make a nice statement or two. The 'Specifics of the Analyses' are more like Ole Gunnar Solskjaer; if you're ever in trouble they'll be there with the answers, whilst the 'References' are your Michel Vorm; they'll provide reassurances if you ever need them but most of the time you can leave them where they are. And finally, the Postface is a bit like when Antonio Conte brings on Michy Batshuayi in the 93rd minute – short, sweet, but feel free to leave early as you won't miss much.

Like all good football matches, each chapter will start with a warm-up; a short introduction that explains how I came to analysing that specific topic. Following that, the line-ups will be announced. These are the methods I've used to answer the question, and will show how I've gone about collecting and analysing the data. Next is the match! Here I'll present to you the results from the analysis, and highlight the important bits (a bit like they do on *Match of the Day)*. Finally each chapter will end with a post-match interview; a conclusion that should hopefully wrap up the topic in a nice neat bow.

A word of warning for all the readers out there who are far smarter than I am (that will be most of you): these analyses are not water-tight answers! They are simply my way of providing an alternative (and data-driven) perspective on a variety of football debates. There will be flaws to each and every one of them. Hopefully I will justify, or at least acknowledge, many of these, but if I don't...well, think of me a bit like the referee: just yell at the book, bellow that I don't know what I'm doing, then begrudgingly carry on reading.

Contents

1. Too Big To Go Down

The Warm-Up

In 2016, Leicester City completed the greatest shock in the history of sport when they won the Premier League title. In an era of unrivalled disparity between the big teams and the little teams, Leicester held off the likes of Arsenal, Tottenham Hotspur, and the two Manchester giants who between them had combined to spend over £380 million during the season (not to mention then-holders Chelsea who themselves spent £77 million)[1]. Fast-forward nine months and the fairy tale was well and truly over. Leicester were in the middle of a relegation battle, and had sacked their hero Claudio Ranieri. Only one side has ever won the top division and then followed it up with the dreaded drop – but that was Manchester City way back in 1938 when football was very different from what it is today. Was it to be, that the champions of England – a team who made it to the quarter-finals of Europe's elite competition – were about to get relegated to a league in which they'd be playing the likes of Burton Albion and Bristol City? As it turns out, the answer was no. Leicester, in the end, were simply copying the 2016 Chelsea blueprint for how to defend a title: the blues very briefly flirted with the drop that season before eventually navigating their way to 10th place. But Chelsea – unlike Leicester – never *really* looked like getting relegated. With the likes of Courtois, Willian, Hazard, and Diego Costa how could they? They were *too big to go down*. Or were they? Is there even such a thing as being too big to go down? And who is the biggest team to ever be relegated from the Premier League? These questions now have answers...

The Line Ups

76 teams have been relegated from the Premier League dating back to its inception in 1992/93. Note, the term 'teams' refers to each individual season, not each individual 'club'. For example, three Hull City teams have been relegated; the 2010 team, the 2015 team, and the 2017 team. To gauge the size of each team, their league positions from the 46 seasons prior to being relegated was compared. 46 seasons was the maximum number possible due to a need to ensure equal sample sizes. Whilst reliable records go back longer than 46 years for recently relegated teams, for the teams who were relegated in 1993, anything over 46 seasons runs into the World War 2, when the top divisions were not played.

These positions act as scores for each team, with *lower scores indicating bigger teams*. For example, finishing 7th in the Premier League the season prior to relegation gives a score of 7, whilst finishing 17th in the Premier League the season prior to relegation gives a score of 17. Finishing 10th in the second tier would give a score of 30 (or 32 back when the top tier contained 22 teams). Any finish below the second tier is given a score of 50 regardless of position finished.

Furthermore (as seems appropriate), each season is not weighted equally, with more recent seasons being given greater importance. In the first season prior to relegation, scores are multiplied by a factor of 50, and then for each season preceding this decreases by 1. For example, in 2015, Newcastle United finished 15th, then 10th in 2014, 16th in 2013, 5th in 2012, and 12th in 2011. Their score over this 5 year period would be (15x50) + (10x49) + (16x48) + (5x47) + (12x46) = 2795. This continues all the way down to the 46th season prior to relegation, which has a multiplication factor of 5.

The Match

The table below shows the top 20 biggest teams to have been relegated from the Premier League. The full table of all 76 relegated (along with the current Premier League teams and other notable cases interjected) can be found in the 'Specifics of the Analyses' chapter.

Rank	Team	Year	Score
1	Aston Villa	2016	14335
2	Leeds United	2004	15705
3	Nottingham Forest	1997	16599
4	Nottingham Forest	1999	16911
5	Newcastle United	2016	17591
6	Nottingham Forest	1993	17624
7	Newcastle United	2009	18209
8	Manchester City	1996	18351
9	West Ham United	2003	18517
10	Southampton	2005	18524
11	West Ham United	2011	18929
12	Coventry City	2001	22234
13	Manchester City	2001	22776
14	Ipswich Town	2002	23339
15	Ipswich Town	1995	24397
16	Leicester City	2002	25260
17	Leicester City	2004	25425
18	Blackburn Rovers	2012	25548
19	Sheffield Wednesday	2000	25975
20	Middlesbrough	2009	26041

Lower scores indicate bigger teams

A Shock Number One? The analysis suggests that the 2016 Aston Villa side were the biggest to ever be relegated from the Premier League, followed by the 2004 Leeds side, 1997 and 1999 Nottingham Forest sides, and then the 2016 Newcastle United team. This may be slightly surprising, given that Leeds won the old first division in 1992 and were in the Champions League as recently as 2001, but by the time they were relegated in 2004 they had only been in the top flight for 14 consecutive seasons. Compare that to Aston Villa who, until their relegation last year, had been playing in the top division for 28 straight seasons, and the result becomes a little more expected. This factor also explains the perhaps strange inclusion of Coventry City in 12th place. Whilst they may never have been battling towards the upper reaches of the Premier League (or First Division) they were in the top flight for 33 consecutive years before finally succumbing to the drop in 2001. They now play in the fourth tier of English football.

The next table lists the 2017/18 Premier League clubs (what is, as of this writing, the *current* season) and their scores, were they to be relegated come May 2018. In essence, this table can also be seen as simply listing which teams are the biggest in the league!

Rank	Team	Year	Score
1	Manchester United	2018	4456
2	Arsenal	2018	5025
3	Liverpool	2018	5152
4	Chelsea	2018	9918
5	Tottenham Hotspur	2018	10143
6	Everton	2018	11652
7	Manchester City	2018	16487
8	Newcastle United	2018	18070

9	West Ham United	2018	18411
10	Southampton	2018	23096
11	West Bromwich Albion	2018	28976
12	Leicester City	2018	29703
13	Crystal Palace	2018	33126
14	Stoke City	2018	33471
15	Watford	2018	37566
16	Burnley	2018	45330
17	Swansea City	2018	47293
18	Brighton & Hove Albion	2018	51035
19	Huddersfield Town	2018	55364
20	AFC Bournemouth	2018	56370

Lower scores indicate bigger teams

Sir Alex Ferguson's achievements at Manchester United are such that even finishes of 6th, 5th, 4th, and 7th in the past four seasons cannot move them from top of the table. They remain a slightly bigger team than Arsenal, who again benefit from considerable success not so long ago. Liverpool – yet to win the Premier League – make up the top 3, in large part due to their accomplishments in the 1970s and 1980s. From 1973 to 1991 the club only failed to make the top two once. Compare this to current powerhouses Chelsea (who played in the second tier for 8 seasons and had a highest finish of 5th during that time) and Manchester City (who had an average league finish of 15th in the same period) and you can see why the top 3 sit so far ahead of all the other Premier League clubs.

Younger football fans may be surprised to see recently promoted Newcastle United in 8th place, whilst AFC Bournemouth – despite being in the Premier League for the past two seasons – sit bottom, behind the two other newcomers Brighton & Hove Albion and Huddersfield Town.

Other Highlights

- Had the 2015/16 Premier League winners Leicester City been relegated as champions – as it looked like they might in February 2017 – they wouldn't even be in the top 20 "biggest" teams to have gone down…in fact, they wouldn't even be the biggest Leicester City team to go down – with the 2002 Leicester side markedly superior!

- Whilst the 2004 Leeds team is the second biggest to ever be relegated, the 1993 side went into the inaugural Premier League season as champions of England having won the last ever First Division title in 1992. They ended up finishing 17th, just 2 points above the drop, yet if they had been relegated the champions would only have been the 12th biggest side to have done so.

- Of the 20 current Premier League clubs, only six would be bigger than the 2016 Aston Villa team if they were relegated in 2018. Neither Manchester United (Score of 4456), Arsenal (5025), Liverpool (5152), Chelsea (9918), Tottenham Hotspur (10143), or Everton (11652) are likely to "achieve" that feat though. Interestingly, if Manchester City – home of Guardiola, Kompany, De Bruyne, Aguero, and co. – were to somehow end up in the bottom three, they would be only the third biggest team to ever get relegated from the Premier League, with a score of 16487.

- As alluded to in the 'Warm-Up', perhaps Chelsea *were* too big to go down in 2015/16…though it never looked truly likely (the lowest they sunk was 16th place just prior to Christmas), had Chelsea been relegated, they would have done so with a score of 10453 – making them the biggest team to go down by some margin.

- Two other teams could have realistically taken Aston Villa's crown as the biggest team to go down in the Premier League era. Tottenham finished 14th in 2004 and had been in the relegation zone as late as January of that year. Had they gone down their score would have been 12025 – again, considerably lower than the 14335 of the 2016 Aston Villa team. Even bigger than the 2004 Tottenham team was the 1998 Everton team (score of 11485). They finished in 17th in 1998 and survived only by goal difference.

- The smallest team to go down (if there is such a thing?!) was the 2011 Blackpool side, who had a score of 57308. The next closest competitors for that crown were the 2001 Bradford City side (55929) and the 1994 Swindon Town team (55041). Were AFC Bournemouth to be relegated in 2018, they would be the second smallest team to go down (with a score of 56370), whilst if Huddersfield Town make a swift return to the Championship they would be the third smallest (score of 55364).

The Post-Match Interview

The answer to the question "Who is the biggest club to have been relegated from the Premier League?" is clearly subjective dependent upon the criteria you use. In this case, previous league position was the key statistic, however, people make their opinions on a wider variety of reasons than just that. The speed of a club's decline is likely a large factor (Leeds managed to fall from grace pretty quickly...), along with trophies won (Nottingham Forest are two-time European champions...), fan-base (52,000-attendance at St James Park would suggest

Newcastle...), and maybe even a London-centric bias (West-Ham anyone..?). Nevertheless, using just one piece of evidence leads us to the choice of Aston Villa; a team who's decline was moderately quick having finished 6th in 2010, are one-time European champions, can bring in 42,000 fans to Villa Park, and are slightly closer to London than the other options. Seams about right.

2. Value for Money

The Warm-Up

Let's start things off by saying that no player in this modern era of football is worth what is paid for them (or *to* them for that matter). The fact that West Ham's signing of Andre Ayew – scorer of 12 goals in 34 league games for Swansea City – cost roughly (taking inflation into account) the same as the Premier League's greatest ever striker, Alan Shearer – scorer of 260 goals in 441 league games for both Blackburn Rovers and Newcastle United – should tell you all you need to know on that matter. That said, it is what it is. There is no turning back on the madness that is football finances, but what can be done, is compare the relative value of these signings.

Over the past two years, perhaps no signings have produced more debate in the English game than that of John Stones and Raheem Sterling. The Telegraph stated that the transfer fee for Sterling had "caused outrage, confusion and isolated outbreaks of humour"[1], whilst John Stones' value was labelled "startling"[2]. However, are these fair reflections (ignoring also that the players themselves are not the ones dictating these numbers) on the two transfers?

The Line Ups

Two things often get overlooked which are important to consider in this debate: longevity, and nationality. Longevity –

or how long a player will be able to contribute for – is hugely important. Just like you would expect to pay more for a brand new car than one with 20,000 miles on it, so you should expect to pay more for a player at the start of his career than one at the end (or even middle) of it. Teams pay for potential. Nationality, on the other hand, is key because of the regulations governing football squads. Premier League teams are required to have at least eight home-grown players in their 25 man squad, meaning English players are a necessity, and not just a preference. Given the breadth of footballing talent around the world, and the global appeal of the Premier League, the proportion of adequate English players available is relatively small, thus making them more valuable.

Accounting for these factors in football transfers is fairly straightforward; we simply determine 1) how many (meaningful) years a player has left, and 2) decide upon a fair deduction for their eligibility to EU regulations, to calculate a *cost per season* for each player. Comparing this new value should give a fairer reflection on each transfer.

The first part of this equation – how many years a player has left – can be estimated based on data showing the mean age of Premier League footballers. Position played needs to be taken into account here, as clearly goalkeepers tend to have longer shelf lives than defenders, who in turn usually last longer than midfielders and forwards. A quick (ish!) analysis of Premier League starting 11's from the 2015/16 season showed the average age of each position to be:

Goalkeepers – 28.8, Defenders – 27.5, Midfielders – 26.2, Forwards – 25.0

Using a bit of stats, we can work out where 95% of these players fall amongst this range, and therefore produce a good value to use for our estimate of a player's career length. This leaves us with a goalkeeper's longevity being until age 36, a defender's until 34, a midfielders until 32, and a forward's also until 32.

The second part of this equation is a little trickier and involves subjective judgement. How much more valuable is an EU eligible player? Or, put another way: how much does being English add to the cost of a player in the Premier League? There is no set number for this, and it is difficult to even find a ball-park figure when searching the internet, merely that it is "pushing up transfer fees for those types of players"[3]. One possible way to estimate this is by comparing two similar players. Raheem Sterling and Anthony Martial both made big money moves to very rich, very high-profile English clubs in 2015. Both were very young, and both play as wingers/forwards. But the transfer fee paid for Martial was only 80% that paid for Sterling...does that mean being English adds 20% to a player's value? Possibly, though it should be noted that Sterling had played for England numerous times before his transfer, whereas Martial had yet to win his first international cap, so maybe this is over-stating it a little. A figure of 15% is a bit more conservative and may be a bit more accurate. As mentioned, this part of the equation does involve some subjective opinion, but 15% seems about right – some may argue it undervalues it, whilst others could argue it overvalues it.

Now that these two overlooked factors have been considered, and the values for our equation determined, the debates surrounding the Stones and Sterling transfers can be viewed in a fairer light. To do this, comparisons will be made with the ten highest transfer fees to the Premier League from the 2015/16 and 2016/17 Premier League seasons.

- 'Cost per Season' formula for English players: (Transfer fee – 15% of Transfer fee) / Years Left
- 'Cost per Season' formula for non-English players: Transfer fee / Years Left

The Match

As the table below shows, Raheem Sterling and John Stones make up the 3rd and 4th most expensive transfers to the Premier League in the 2015/16 and 2016/17 seasons. But when we take into account our two important factors of longevity and nationality, on a cost per season basis, they now only rank 12th and 15th, respectively. This contrast can be seen more clearly in the two subsequent graphs.

Rank	Player	Age	Transfer Fee	Years Left	English ?	Cost per Season	New Rank
1	Paul Pogba	23	£89.25	9		£9.92	1
2	Kevin De Bruyne	24	£62.90	8		£7.86	2
3	Raheem Sterling	20	£53.13	12	Yes	£3.76	12
4	John Stones	22	£47.26	12	Yes	£3.35	15
5	Anthony Martial	19	£42.50	13		£3.27	17
6	Leroy Sane	20	£42.50	12		£3.54	13
7	Christian Benteke	24	£39.53	8		£4.94	7
8	Granit Xhaka	23	£38.25	9		£4.25	9
9	Nicolas Otamendi	27	£37.91	7		£5.42	6
10	Henrikh Mkhitaryan	27	£35.70	5		£7.14	3
11	Sadio Mane	24	£35.02	8		£4.38	8
12	Roberto Firmino	23	£34.85	9		£3.87	11
13	Shkodran Mustafi	24	£34.85	10		£3.49	14
14	Michy Batshuayi	22	£33.15	10		£3.32	16
15	David Luiz	29	£32.73	5		£6.55	4
16	Eric Bailly	22	£32.30	12		£2.69	19
17	Morgan Schneiderlin	25	£29.75	7		£4.25	9
18	Memphis Depay	21	£28.90	11		£2.63	20
19	Heung-Min Son	23	£25.50	9		£2.83	18
20	Pedro	28	£22.95	4		£5.74	5

Light blue shades indicate transfers from the 2015/16 season; light red shades indicate transfers from the 2016/17 season. Transfer fee and cost per season are in millions.

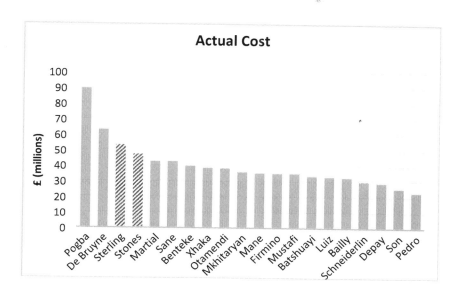

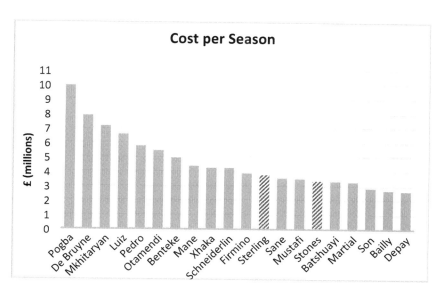

Other Highlights

- Chelsea's Pedro may have been the cheapest purchase of the 20 players analysed, but because he was 28 at the time of the transfer (and therefore only has four more seasons "left in the tank") his cost per season actually makes him the 5th most expensive!
- There's an odd element of symmetry regarding two of the centre-backs analysed. John Stones' old ranking was 4th, but his new ranking is 15th, whereas David Luiz's old ranking was 15th but his new ranking is 4th.
- Manchester City's signing of Gabriel Jesus – at £27.2 million – didn't quite crack the top 10 from 2016/17. However, had the Brazilian sensation been included, at 19 years of age his cost per season would have been £2.09 million. This would have made him the cheapest of all in the new ranking.
- 324 players were signed by Premier League clubs in the two seasons of 2015/16 and 2016/17. 65 were English. That's 20%. After Sterling and Stones, the next most expensive Englishman was Jordan Ibe who went from Liverpool to AFC Bournemouth for £15.3 million – 42nd highest in this period.

The Post-Match Interview

The transfers of Sterling and Stones, then, are not as ridiculous as they first appear. Or probably more aptly, they are at least *less* ridiculous than some of the other transfers that seem to receive fewer instances of negative publicity. So why is it that little is made of the fees paid for Mkhitaryan, David Luiz, or Pedro? Is it that maybe the average football fan/media is less knowledgeable of players not currently playing in England, and therefore refrains from immediate judgement? Or perhaps fans and the media in England hold some sort of odd grudge against fellow compatriots "making it"? Maybe it's less to do with nationality and more to do with age: potential is hard to fathom, whereas proven ability is easy to see.

None of this is to say that people aren't entitled to their opinions. Opinions are what makes the game great, and if you believe that Sterling and Stones aren't worth what Manchester City paid for them, then that's great. But for media reports to state that the transfers caused "confusion" and were "startling" is strange, because no matter whether you disagree with them or not, the reasoning behind them – their age and nationality – is completely logical.

3. Grinding Out a Result

The Warm-Up

Grinding out a result is the hallmark of champions according to many football observers. That ability to eke out a win by the odd goal when not playing as well as expected, or perhaps even warranted, is what separates title winners from title also-rans. Leicester City were the masters of it in their triumphant 2015-16 season, at one point winning 1-0 in 5 of their 6 games from February 27th to April 3rd. Jose Mourinho sides have apparently got a penchant for it too[1], whilst many would say that some of Sir Alex Ferguson's Manchester United sides actually invented the whole concept. In fact, the legendary Scottish manager reportedly believed that such results were "part of the DNA that makes up champions"[2]. A more respected advocate would be hard to find.

It's a nice thought. The idea that what separates truly great sides from their close competitors is their ability to come together when times get tough and battle through for the victory. But actually, it doesn't really make that much sense. The best team in a league is surely more likely to dismantle opponents by 2, 3, 4, or more goals, not scrape by every match. The odd close call, yes. But not the week-in-week-out occurrences that we are led to believe defines a championship winning team.

And this relates to the major problem with many of the pseudo-analyses conducted on the topic: they often just compare the *frequency* of such wins[3]. The most common victory in the English Premier League (whatever position a team is in) is 1-0 or 2-1[4]. Given that the team who wins the league is the one that has the most points – and therefore most likely has the most wins – this creates a huge problem. What is needed is to compare the *percentage* of victories that a team wins by a one goal margin, not the *frequency*. This accounts for the champions being a simply better team than others, and is a much better indicator of the ability to "grind out a result".

The Line Ups

The teams finishing in the top 6 positions of the English Premier League in the 22 seasons between 1995/96 and 2016/17 were used in the analysis. Prior to this, the Premier League had 22 teams, rather than 20, and therefore inclusion of such data may have resulted in unfair comparisons. The frequency of 1 goal, 2 goal, 3 goal, and 4 or more goal (4+) winning margins were found for each of these teams. These were then converted into percentages of their total number of wins. For example, in 2015/16, 14 of Leicester's 23 victories were by a 1 goal margin. This equates to 60.9%. It is also important to note that in this analysis, *all* 1 goal margins will be included, i.e., 1-0, 2-1, 3-2, 4-3, and so on. Whilst this may seem clear, it is important to reiterate given that many other analyses on the topic have tended to only use the 1-0 margin as an indicator, whilst neglecting results such as 2-1 and 3-2. This is flawed given that there is no reason to believe that a 4-3 victory is any less of a "grind" than a 1-0 victory.

The Match

First Half: 1 goal margin

Going against the commonly held belief, champions do not "grind out a result" more than their close competitors. In fact, they do so considerably less than teams that finish 5th and 6th in the league, and at about the same rate as those that finish 2nd, 3rd, and 4th.

The most 1 goal margin of victories ever recorded in a season was 16 by Manchester United in their title triumphs of 2008/09 and 2012/13. However, the percentages of each (57.1% both times) were not the highest. That record belongs to the 2004/05 6th placed Bolton Wanderers side, who, out of 16 victories, won 13 by a single goal, equating to 81.3%. The highest percentage by a champion team is 60.9% set by the Leicester City side in 2015/16. Incredibly, when Arsenal finished 3rd in 1996/97, only 2 of their 19 victories (10.5%) were by a 1 goal margin.

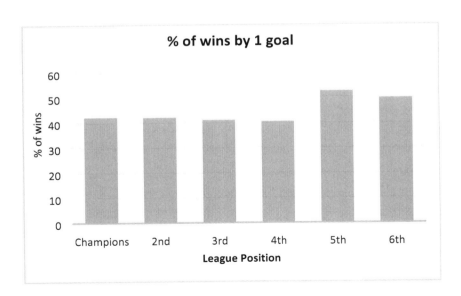

Second Half: 2 goal margin

Within the 2 goal data we see that those finishing 3rd, 4th, and 5th have a slightly higher percentage of their victories by a 2 goal margin than the champions, 2nd place, and 6th place. These disparities are only very small though, with the difference between the highest (5th place) and lowest (6th place) just 4.2%.

The same Arsenal team mentioned above hold the record for highest percentage of victories by a 2 goal margin at 73.7% - a staggering achievement considering that next highest percentage is just 61%, set by Manchester United in 2016/17. Fierce rivals Tottenham Hotspur were next, with 55% of their victories coming by 2 goals in 2011/12.

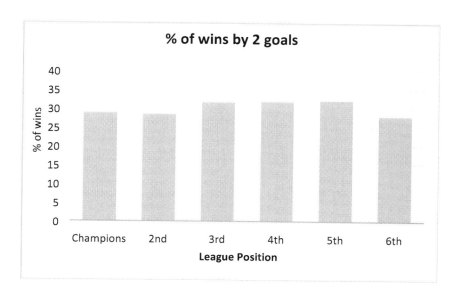

Extra Time: 3 goal margin

As a percentage of total victories, 3rd and 4th placed teams achieve more by a 3 goal margin than do champions, 2nd placed, and 6th placed teams. 3 goal margins account for only 10.1% of all wins for 5th placed teams; almost half that of 3rd placed teams.

It is not uncommon for teams to finish in the top 6 without winning a single game by a 3 goal margin, in fact, it has occurred 8 times over the past 21 seasons. Chelsea, Aston Villa, and Tottenham Hotspur have all done this twice, with Leeds United and Everton doing so once. 7 out of these 8 instances involved teams finished 4th, 5th, or 6th; only the 2007/08 Chelsea team finished higher (2nd).

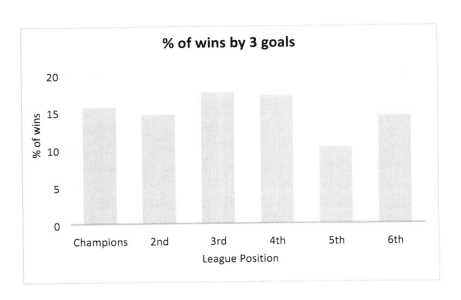

Penalties: 4+ goal margin

It is in the 4+ data that we see why champions and 2nd placed teams had a lower percentage of their victories by 1 goal than 5th and 6th placed teams, and a lower percentage of their victories by 3 goals than 3rd and 4th placed teams. Champions (and 2nd placed teams) are more likely to dominate a team in their victory. Given that the champions win an average of 26 games per season, the 13.7% of victories achieved by 4 or more goals means that almost four teams each year are on the receiving end of a very lopsided result from these teams. The same is true of teams who finish runners-up, as their slightly fewer average wins per season (24) is made up for by a slightly higher percentage of 4+ goal margins (15.1%).

Manchester City may have only just made it into the top 4 in 2015/16, but they had the highest percentage of victories by a 4+ margin recorded by a top 6 team over the last 22 seasons, with 31.2%. This was the same percentage as their wins by a 1 goal margin, meaning they were just as likely scrape to victory as they were to coast to one. The 2016/17 Tottenham Hotspur follow closely behind, with 30.8% of their victories being by 4 or more goals – ending the season with a 6-1 and 7-1 win certainly helped towards this. It should be noted though, that this Tottenham team, as well as the 2009/10 Chelsea team, did record two more 4+ victory margins than Manchester City in 2015/16. Interestingly a team finishing as champions or in 2nd place have never failed to record a 4+ victory during a season.

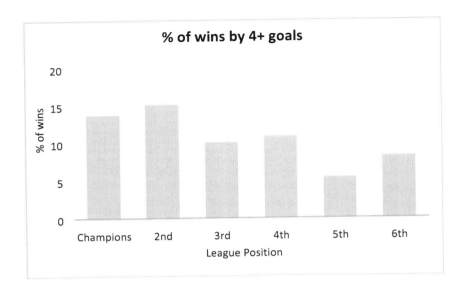

The Post-Match Interview

Data 1-0 Cliché. The idea that champions grind out a result does not show up in the data, and oddly, as mentioned before, when it is given some thought it doesn't make any intuitive sense either. Which makes it strange why it even became a cliché in the first place. A much more apt cliché would be "champions and runners-up dominate matches", though that does not roll off the tongue quite so well.

As with many of the clichés that are covered in this book, there is likely to be some cognitive bias at work. One such bias that may be particularly relevant here is the narrative fallacy. The narrative fallacy essentially refers to our predisposition to retrospectively look for – and find – links between facts and information in order to come up with a coherent story[5]. So perhaps when we see a team who are top of the league win by the odd goal against a team much worse than them (when we should really expect them to win by much more), we recall other instances of this too – a confirmation bias. We then put together a picture of this being common – or even essential – for a title-winning team. We maybe even justify this by pointing out the players who are pivotal in these "grinded out results" – N'Golo Kante for Leicester, Roy Keane for Manchester United, Claude Makelele for Chelsea, and so on. If someone told you, back in 2000, that Arsenal had "grinded out a 1-0 victory" over Manchester United; would you picture Patrick Vieira or Thierry Henry? Maybe I'm in the minority (and this would be an interesting idea to study) but I would predict most would say Vieira. Yet Arsenal did grind out a victory over Manchester United back in 2000, and the goal that won it? A flick, a pirouette, and a looping volley over the head of the goalkeeper from 25 yards out by Henry.

4. The Most Competitive League in the World

The Warm-Up

It has been said that "clichés come into common use because they are very often true"[1]. A cliché perhaps (understandably) confined to only the English game is the statement that the Premier League "is the most competitive league in the world". This common perception is often reported when one of the relegation-threatened teams defeats a title-challenger, with the belief that this occurs more frequently than in the other major European leagues.

This is a reasonable belief to hold for a number of reasons. First and foremost, for the simple matter that Leicester City managed to win the Premier League in 2015/16 despite sitting 20th in the league with 7 games to go of the previous season. Leicester's triumph also made them the fourth different winner of the title in the last four seasons – something that hasn't happened in any of the other top 20 European leagues in that timespan (and potentially more as I gave up checking after 20). Furthermore, audiences generally want to watch (and thus companies are willing to pay for) *competitive* sport; and there is no doubt that the Premier League receives substantially greater TV revenues than any other league in the world[2]. All these factors make a strong argument for the idea that the Premier League is the most competitive league in the world, but is this backed up by the data?

The Line Ups

There are two main ways in which we can measure competitiveness: the first is via points spreads across the season, and the second is via frequency of certain winning margins.

For the first method, the key is the difference in ability between the top team and the bottom team. The smaller the difference, the greater the competitiveness. This ability can be determined using the end-of-season point's totals of such teams. For example, in the 2014/15 Premier League season, Chelsea finished 1st with 87 points, whilst Queens Park Rangers finished 20th with 30 points. This 57-point difference was greater than that between Paris Saint-Germain (1st with 83 points) and Lens (20th with 29 points) in France's Ligue 1 during the same season, and therefore we can say that Ligue 1 was *more competitive* than the Premier League that season.

However, rather than using points totals, a better method to use is average points earned per game. The reason for this can be found in the 'Specifics of the Analyses' chapter, but essentially it comes down to ensuring reliable and fair data across the different leagues. The differences in average points earned per game between the top and bottom teams was compared between the English Premier League, the Spanish La Liga, the Italian Serie A, the German Bundesliga, and the French Ligue 1; five leagues commonly referred to as the "top leagues in the world"[3]. It should be noted though, that comparing the data between only the top and bottom teams may not accurately reflect overall league competitiveness, as there may be instances in which one team has been especially dominant (or especially weak) during a season, yet the other 18 (or 16 for the Bundesliga) may have been very competitive. To account for this, we can compare the difference between the top team and bottom team (1 v 1), top two teams and bottom two teams (2 v

2), top three teams and bottom three teams (3 v 3), and top four teams and bottom four teams (4 v 4).

For the second method, competitiveness is measured within individual matches, as opposed to cumulatively across a season. This analysis is much simpler than for the one above, as it only involves calculating and comparing the frequency of victories by 4 or more goals for each of the five major leagues. A greater frequency of such results likely indicates less competitive matches, and therefore less competitive leagues.

The Match

First Half: Points Spread

And the most competitive league in the world is…the French Ligue 1! The English Premier League isn't even close. Of the five major leagues in the world, overall the English Premier League is the second *least* competitive, behind only the Italian Serie A. In fact, it is actually slightly less competitive than its Italian counterpart when only comparing the top and bottom 4 teams. This is a far cry from what the media (at least in England) would have you believe.

Whilst the decision to analyse across a number of team ranges (i.e., 1 v 1 to 4 v 4) was based on sound logic, the results show that league competitiveness is relatively stable across all comparisons. The French Ligue 1 is the most competitive by a considerable distance, followed by the German Bundesliga and Spain's La Liga clear in 2nd and 3rd, and then the English Premier League and Italian Serie A bringing up the rear in 4th and 5th. It is only in the 4 v 4 comparison where there is any real change; with the reversal of the Premier League and Serie A as previously mentioned.

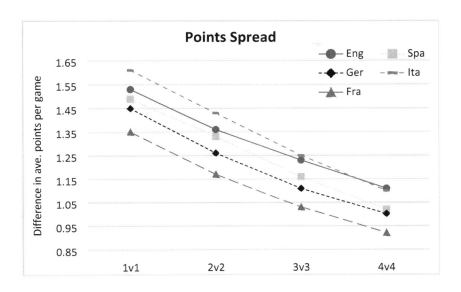

Difference in Average Points per Game (combining all ranges)				
English Premier League	Spanish La Liga	German Bundesliga	Italian Serie A	French Ligue 1
1.31	1.25	1.21	1.35	1.12

Second Half: Winning Margins

Interestingly, when using Winning Margins as the measure of competitiveness, the picture painted by the data is considerably different. Remarkably, the Italian Serie A is now the *most* competitive league, with the fewest number of lopsided matches in three of the six seasons, as well as overall. The French Ligue 1 performs admirably again; whilst it had the most lopsided matches in the 2016/17 season, it had the fewest in 2011/12, and the second fewest overall. The English Premier

League comes next, though it was able to claim bragging rights in one season – 2014/15 – when just 13 matches were won by 4 or more goals. Germany's Bundesliga – though very similar to the Premier League between 2012 and 2014 – finishes as the second *least* competitive. By far and away the *least* competitive league, however, was Spain's La Liga. In five of the six seasons analysed, La Liga had considerably more 4+ goal winning margins than any other league. It almost doubled the closest challengers to that title in 2013, and overall finished with 62 more than the "second placed" German Bundesliga, and 105 more than the Italian Serie A!

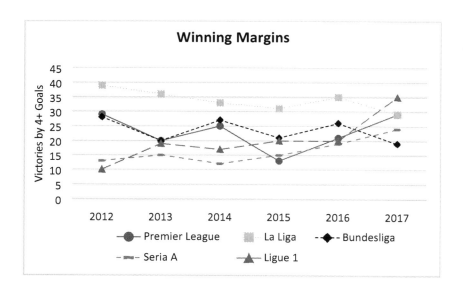

Total Number of 4+ Goal Winning Margins (2011/12 – 2016/17)				
English Premier League	Spanish La Liga	German Bundesliga	Italian Serie A	French Ligue 1
137	203	141	98	121

Other Highlights

- English Premier League: Despite both teams having an average league position over the last 6 seasons that would leave them outside of the top 4, Tottenham Hotspur and Liverpool have the second (17) and third (16) highest number of 4+ victory margins in the Premier League, respectively. Interestingly, there are 14 instances recorded by teams that no longer play in the Premier League (Fulham 3, Sunderland 3, Aston Villa 2, Bolton Wanderers 2, Hull City 2, Norwich City 1, and Wigan Athletic 1).

- Spanish La Liga: Only one team set to play in La Liga in 2017/18 has *not* been on the receiving end of a 4+ victory margin over the past 6 seasons: Barcelona. Even the mighty Real Madrid have fallen victim once; in a 4-0 drubbing at the Camp Nou in the 2015/16 El Classico. Note, this was written prior to the Segunda Division (Spanish second tier) playoffs, however, of the four teams involved in this, only two – Tenerife and Cadiz – could invalidate this statistic...though neither will have actually played in La Liga over that 6 season time period anyway!

- German Bundesliga: Based on this data, Bayern Munich and Borussia Dortmund are marginally more dominant in the Bundesliga than Barcelona and Real Madrid are in La Liga. The German clubs account for 55.7% of their leagues 4+ victory margins compared to 54.2% for the Spanish giants.

- Italian Serie A: To support its claim as most competitive league, Serie A didn't have a "whipping boy" over the past 6 seasons (a team that was on the receiving end of a lopsided result substantially more than other teams). 27 different teams were dealt a 4+ defeat. Given that the Italian league had 98 instances in total, this works out at an average of 3.6 instances per team. By comparison, La Liga averaged 7.0 instances per team, the Bundesliga; 5.3, the Premier League; 4.7, and Ligue 1; 4.3.

- French Ligue 1: In the three seasons between 2011/12 and 2013/14 there were no victories by more than 5+ goals in Ligue 1. In the same time, La Liga had 10, the Premier League had 9, the Bundesliga had 5, and Serie A had 3. However, the largest victory margin across all leagues over the past six seasons *was* in Ligue 1, when Paris Saint-Germain beat Troyes 9-0 in 2015/16.

The Post-Match Interview

In 2016, Leicester City won the English Premier League title. It was a remarkable achievement that proved – if it were even needed – that the Premier League is the most competitive league in the world. Where else could a team who finished 14th the season before, and with title-odds of 5,000-1, go on to finish above free-spending giants like Manchester United, Manchester City, Chelsea, and Arsenal? Yet looking back at it all, they did so comfortably. It wasn't actually that competitive a league season. They ended 10 points clear of second place, and 15 points clear of fourth. Combine this with one of the poorest Premier League seasons on record at the other end of the table by Aston Villa, and you have a season that was less competitive than Spain's La Liga and Italy's Serie A.

This misperception of the Premier League is backed up by real-world data. In neither the Points Spread or Winning Margins analyses did the English Premier League come out on top. Rather, the French Ligue 1 can probably best claim this crown, given that it was the most competitive league as determined by Points Spread, and was the second most competitive league as determined by Winning Margins. Least competitive is a little trickier to work out...depending on the method use, you could actually argue the case for any of the other four countries.

These results initially appear like they are providing contrasting conclusions. How can it be that Serie A has the fewest lopsided results over the past 5 seasons but the largest points disparity between top and bottom teams? Likewise, La Liga has by far the highest amount of lopsided results, but a relatively moderate points disparity. Perhaps what we are seeing is indicative of the style of football adopted by certain teams. Juventus for example (winner of Serie A for the past 6 seasons by an average of 10 points, including one in which they went unbeaten), may not thrash teams, but rather, get into comfortable positions in matches which they are then content to hold on to. By contrast, the likes of Barcelona and Real Madrid may do the opposite; get into comfortable leads but then attempt to punish their opponents further. This may result in considerably more 4+ margins of victory, but also more instances in which they drop points (which would subsequently reduce their points disparity with the rest of the league). This theory could be worth examining in the future.

So why is it that we have the belief that the Premier League is the most competitive league in the world? Well, the reasons outlined in the 'Warm-Up' provide solid arguments (which can be linked to the psychological phenomenon discussed in Chapter 11's 'He's Come Back to Haunt Them" analysis), however, there may be a simpler reason behind it. The cliché, originated and delivered by the English footballing media, tends to benefit one group of people more than any other: the English footballing media.

5. Why Rooney Should Blame Ronaldo

The Warm-Up

As of this writing, Wayne Rooney looks all but certain to leave Manchester United before the start of the 2017/18 season. The footballing powerhouse of China seems the most likely destination according to the bookies, with the retirement home that is the MLS another option. This is a man who won't turn 32 until the end of October. That's a year and a half younger than Atletico Madrid's Fernando Torres, three years younger than AFC Bournemouth's Jermain Defoe (who has reportedly just signed a 3-year deal worth £65,000 per week[1]), and four years younger than Zlatan Ibrahimovic; a man who just bagged 17 Premier League goals in 28 games. This is also a man who recently surpassed the legendary Sir Bobby Charlton to become Manchester United's greatest ever goal scorer; a feat he achieved in 215 fewer matches. This needs to be repeated so as to not understate it. Manchester United: one of the world's most iconic football clubs, who have had the likes of George Best, Denis Law, and Eric Cantona wear the famous red shirt, have Wayne Rooney as their *greatest ever goal scorer.* Oh, and there's also the small matter that he is England's leading goal scorer too (above the likes of Jimmy Greaves, Gary Lineker, and Alan Shearer), and England's leading outfield appearance maker (ahead of players such as Bobby Moore, Bryan Robson, and Steven Gerrard). And yet despite all this, no player probably receives more criticism in the media than Rooney[2].

Why is this the case? A large majority of fans may blame Rooney himself. "He didn't live up to his potential" they will say[3]; referencing his impact at Euro 2004 as a sign of what he should have become. This is a fair, albeit harsh, assessment given that he scored 4 goals in 4 games and was named in the UEFA team of the tournament. It's a bit like criticising Gabriel Jesus if he doesn't score 30 goals next season (2017/18), given what he did in his first 10 appearances for Manchester City. Others may point the finger at the media. They over-hyped him back then, like they do with all young English talent. The Guardian, for instance, published an article titled "Is Rooney the new Pele?"[4] That's Pele. Arguably the greatest of all time. Perhaps blame could even be laid at the feet of Sir Alex Ferguson. The Manchester United manager took an 18-year-old boy whose direct running and carefree dribbling terrified defenders, and turned him into a fine player...but one inhibited by a fear of making mistakes. All of these are solid arguments, but there's one person who is never mentioned. One person that has perhaps played a greater role, albeit indirectly, than any of the others listed above. That person is Cristiano Ronaldo.

The Line Ups

To understand why Ronaldo is to blame for the criticism Rooney receives we need to run a short but fairly complicated (for this book!) analysis of data. Below is a table of the goal-scoring achievements of the two players over their careers. For example, in Rooney's first proper season he played for Everton and scored 8 goals (all competitions). In Ronaldo's first proper season he played for Sporting Lisbon and scored 5 goals.

Season	Rooney	Goals	Ronaldo	Goals
1	8	Everton	5	Sporting
2	17	Everton	11	Man Utd
3	34	Man Utd	20	Man Utd
4	53	Man Utd	32	Man Utd
5	76	Man Utd	55	Man Utd
6	94	Man Utd	97	Man Utd
7	114	Man Utd	123	Man Utd
8	148	Man Utd	156	Real Madrid
9	164	Man Utd	209	Real Madrid
10	198	Man Utd	269	Real Madrid
11	214	Man Utd	324	Real Madrid
12	233	Man Utd	375	Real Madrid
13	247	Man Utd	436	Real Madrid
14	262	Man Utd	487	Real Madrid
15	270	Man Utd	529	Real Madrid

There are a number of interesting points to be noted from this table, but the key focus for this analysis is the cut-off point at which the careers of each apparently diverge. A few different seasons could be pinpointed, but season 9 seems the best selection. This was the season that Rooney netted the fewest goals since he was a 17-year-old at Everton, whilst at the same time Ronaldo was establishing himself as an icon at the Bernabeu; scoring 53 in 54 matches. Thus, seasons 1-8 will be termed "pre-split" and seasons 9-15 will be termed "post-split".

The analysis involves producing 3 graphs based on the data in this table:

1. Rooney's goals and Ronaldo's goals each season (both real data). This is termed 'Rooney versus Ronaldo'.
2. Rooney's goals (real data) and Rooney's goals had he lived up to his *pre-split* statistics (projected data). This is termed 'Rooney versus Rooney Projected'.

3. Rooney's goals (real data) and Rooney's goals had he followed Ronaldo's career *post-split* statistics (projected data). This is termed 'Rooney versus Rooney matching Ronaldo'.

The Match

First Half: Rooney versus Ronaldo

This graph simply re-iterates the data in the table previously, and further supports the idea that season 9 is where the two players' careers seem to take different paths. In their first 8 seasons, Rooney (indicated by the solid line) had scored 148 goals, and Ronaldo (indicated by the dashed line) had scored 156 goals. In their last 7 seasons, Rooney has scored 122 goals, and Ronaldo has scored 373 goals. This separation is so large that over their careers, Ronaldo has now scored almost twice as many goals as Rooney.

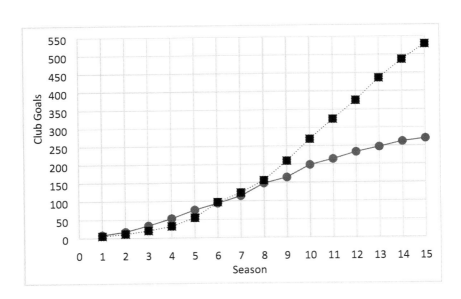

Second Half: Rooney versus Rooney Projected

The solid line is the same as before – this is what Rooney has actually done in his career, goal-wise. The dashed line is his projected goal tally based on *his* data *pre-split*. That is, given his career statistics from seasons 1 to 8, how many goals would we have expected him to score in season 9, 10, 11, and so on? Thus, what we are examining here are the discrepancies (or rather, lack of discrepancies) between the blue and red lines from season 9 onwards. For any stats geeks out there the formula for this works out as: (season*19.857) - 21.357.

The main finding to take from this is that Rooney *has* lived up to his potential – in fact, from season 9 to 14, he very slightly exceeded it! It was only after his 15th season – one in which he scored just 8 goals – that he has fallen behind his projected total. By the end of the 2016/17 season, Rooney should have scored 276 goals based on the first half of his career (a career in which was toe-to-toe with Ronaldo), but his actual total is 270 goals. The idea that Rooney is not as good as he should be is nonsense, at least from a goal-scoring perspective...so the question remains: why do we criticise him so much?

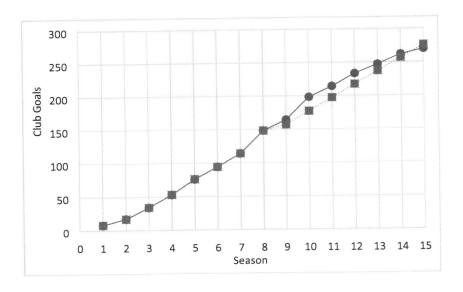

Extra Time: Rooney versus Rooney matching Ronaldo

Again, the solid line show Rooney's actual goals. This time though, the dashed line is based on *Ronaldo's* data *post-split*. That is, given Ronaldo's career statistics from seasons 9 to 14, how many goals would we expect Rooney to score in the same period if he were to have followed the same trajectory? The formula this time is: (Season*55.464) - 343.29. The graph shows that had Rooney somehow managed to keep up with Ronaldo when the Portuguese star morphed into a goal-scoring superhero, we would have expected him to end last season on 489 goals, rather than 270 goals. But rather than this indicate a failure to live up to potential, this graph is much more likely proof that comparisons with perhaps the greatest player to ever grace a football pitch are futile.

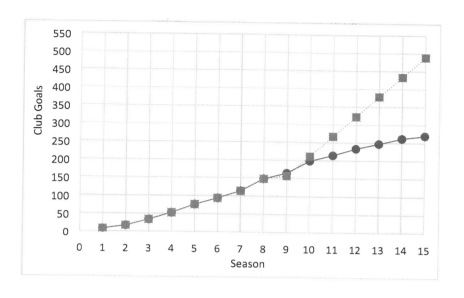

The Post-Match Interview

An extraordinary thing happened in 2010. Cristiano Ronaldo started playing at a level that it was believed only a certain little Argentinian could play at. But rather than marvel at this achievement, it seems that fans and pundits in England use this as a means of criticising Wayne Rooney, even if they do not realise it. It is an easy mistake to make; they were born less than 9 months apart, both billed as the saviours for their country at a time when the previous golden generation was coming to an end, and for 5 years the two played together for one of the biggest clubs in the world. What's more, at Manchester United Rooney more than held his own in his private battle with Ronaldo. To some, he may have even edged it. But then Ronaldo took the next step, and Rooney...continued as expected. To criticise Rooney because he couldn't keep up with a goal-scoring record unlikely to ever be seen again (apart from by that little Argentinian) seems a little unfair, but unfortunately, it is exactly what appears to be happening.

And just to emphasise this harsh reality, below is one final graph that it is hoped may alter some perspectives. It contains the goal scoring data of Wayne Rooney, Cristiano Ronaldo, and three players that arguably are perceived to have a reputation comparative to the Englishman.

Carlos Tevez is a year and a half older than Wayne Rooney and has been capped by Argentina 76 times. They played for Manchester United together between 2007 and 2009, winning the Champions League and back-to-back Premier League titles. Fernando Torres is also a year and a half older than Rooney and has made 110 appearances for Spain, winning the European Championships twice and the World Cup once. For a time, the two were amongst the best forwards the Premier League had to offer. Didier Drogba is a legend at Chelsea, having scored the equaliser and then the winning penalty in their Champions League triumph of 2011/12. He also won the Premier League title and F.A. Cup four times each. Were you to put together a list of the best forwards of the past 15 years, Wayne Rooney, Carlos Tevez, Fernando Torres, and Didier Drogba would probably sit in close proximity to one another.

Yet such a conclusion would be a considerable injustice to Rooney.

As you can see below, Drogba makes a strong case for superiority, but even he falls just short. Tevez and Torres don't even come close. Whatever Chelsea, Manchester City, and Liverpool fans may say – and a lot of neutrals for that matter – Wayne Rooney is the best of the rest. And he has the goal scoring statistics to prove it.

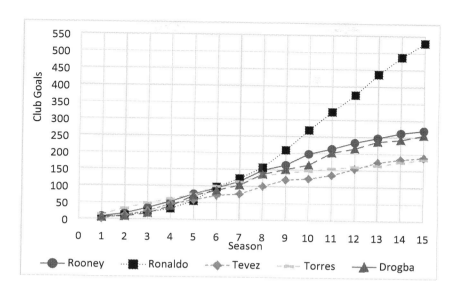

6. Europe: In or Out?

The Warm-Up

On June 23rd 2016, the United Kingdom voted to leave the European Union. The people (well, 51.9% of them) had spoken: Europe was bad.

The same conclusions were made 11 months later when Chelsea cantered to the Premier League title and Liverpool finished 4th, both having had the dubious luxury of not playing European football throughout the season. In fact, the same argument was applied when Leicester City won the league in 2016/17, when Liverpool ended as runners up in 2013/14, and when Tottenham Hotspur, in 2009/10, finished in the top 4 for the first time in 20 years[1]. The reasons, apparently, are clear: playing in Europe means more games. Which means more tired (and potentially more injured) players, and less time to prepare tactically for each game[2]. For instance, Manchester United's Europa League triumph in 2016/17 required them to navigate 15 games, including trips to FC Zorya (Ukraine), Fenerbahce (Turkey), and FC Rostov (Russia). Likewise, Manchester City's run to the Champions League semi-finals in 2015-16 had them playing 12 matches, though only once did they have to venture outside central Europe, when they took on Dynamo Kyiv in the Ukraine. This idea of travel time is also put forward as a hindrance of playing in Europe, with the media often keen to point out how many air miles a team faces when the Champions League and Europa League group stages are drawn. Whether or not such an argument has any validity when analysing real data is a challenge for another time.

Interestingly, the injury records for the two Manchester clubs seem to support this "negative Europe" idea. In 2015/16, Manchester City had 63 injuries[3] in total – the most in the league – whilst in 2016/17, Manchester United had 75 injuries[4] in total – 5th most in the league. The clubs went on to finish 4th and 6th, respectively, which by most people's accounts were both considerable underachievements. These are just two examples though. What does the data say when we include more instances? Will it return the same verdict as the people of the United Kingdom? Or will it conclude that actually, Europe isn't so bad after all?

The Line Ups

Since the 2000/01 season, there have been 34 instances in the Premier League in which a team has gone from playing in Europe one season, to not playing in Europe the next season. Whilst (as always!) there are a multitude of factors that influence performance in football, analysing the *change* in league points between seasons such as these may provide an indicator as to the effect of playing in Europe on a team. Quite nicely for this analysis, in the same time there have also been 34 instances in which the reverse is true (going from not playing in Europe one season to playing in Europe the next season), and again, calculating the *change* in league points between these seasons here may help tell us about the effect of *not* playing in Europe on a team. We can then compare these two changes – from *in to out* and from *out to in* – to see whether it is better to leave Europe or join Europe (admittedly this is where the political analogy breaks down!).

If conventional wisdom is correct, we should find that *in to out* teams see an increase in their league points, whilst *out to in* teams see a decrease in their league points. Note that teams were only included in the analyses if they made it to the first round of European competition. As such, teams that lost in any qualifying phase (such as West Ham United in 2015/16) were not included.

<u>The Match</u>

The graph below shows that the conventional wisdom is indeed backed up by real world data. Going from not playing in Europe to playing in Europe (*out to in*) seems to hinder league performance, with such clubs achieving an average of 7.4 fewer points when they have the added distraction of Champions League or Europa League football. Whilst the difference isn't as great for clubs that go from being in Europe to not being in Europe (*in to out*) there is still an improvement, this time by an average of 2.1 points.

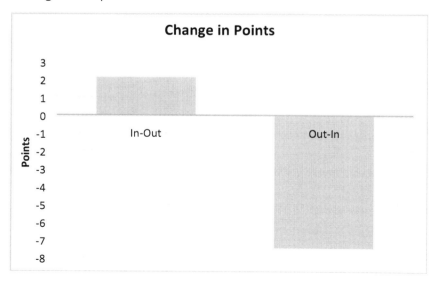

The next graph presents each of the 34 *in to out* instances by the change in league points. Here we see that actually, the change that occurs is fairly negligible. The median value is 0.5, with the mean (the 2.1 identified above) being skewed significantly by the first bar: Chelsea's 43 point improvement from the 2015/16 season to the 2016/17 season. Removing this apparent outlier still results in a positive change in points for the *in to out* teams, but this time by a much smaller 0.9 points.

The final graph below depicts each of the 34 *out to in* instances by the change in league points. Whilst there are some large negative values within the data, none of these would likely be considered an outlier, and this is supported by the median value being -5. Only 9 teams (26%) managed to improve their points haul when going from not playing in Europe to playing in Europe, with Blackburn Rovers in 2002/03 making the biggest increase of 14 points. By comparison, there were 10 teams (29%) which had a decrease of 14 or more points.

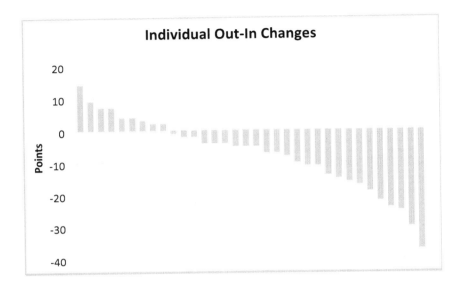

Other Highlights

- Interestingly, the two biggest changes in in points achieved (either *in to out* or *out to in*) have been by the last two Premier League champions. Leicester City followed up their 2015/16 title triumph by earning 37 fewer league points to go with their Champions League adventure, and as already mentioned, Chelsea's 2016/17 title was a result of a 43 point increase.
- There were three instances in which Europe had no impact at all on league points accrued (either *in to out* or *out to in*); Bolton Wanderers in 2006/07, Newcastle United in 2007/08, and Everton in 2015/16 all ended up with the same points total when not playing in Europe

as they did in the previous season when they had played in Europe.

- Newcastle United appear the most times in the analysis. They have gone from *in to out* four times, at an average increase of 5.3 points, and from *out to in* three times at an average decrease of 13.7 points – not a bad reflection on the overall results!

- The Brexit analogy is slightly flawed, given that it was a vote of whether to *remain* in Europe or whether to leave Europe, and not whether to *go into* Europe or leave Europe, as it is in this analysis. Out of interest, though, we can also see the impact of remaining in Europe from a footballing perspective. Teams that stay in Europe in consecutive seasons (*in to in*) tend to decrease their league points by 1.0 points.

The Post-Match Interview

Ironically then, Premier League teams strive all season with the goal of making it into Europe, only to then be disadvantaged the following campaign if they achieve their goal. Clearly many other factors could be at work here (changes in players and managers, improvements or declines by other teams, etc.), but the idea that going from not having European football to having European football (up to 15 additional games as Manchester United have shown) may be detrimental to Premier League performance does make sense. Players will be more tired, and more matches means more opportunities for injuries and less opportunities to prepare for league games. It would be interesting to see whether injury records correlate with these changes, but accurate data for this (aside from the most recent seasons) is difficult to obtain.

With regards the changes from *in to out*, one interesting feature that came out of the data was in which teams seemed to benefit, and which teams actually found it to be unfavourable. The 5 biggest improvements in league points were by Chelsea (2016/17), Liverpool (2013/14), Tottenham Hotspur (2009/10), Manchester City (2009/10), and Liverpool (2016/17), whilst the 5 biggest declines in league points were by Leicester City (2001/02), Blackburn Rovers (2008/09), Southampton (2004/05), Leeds United (2003/04), and Portsmouth (2009/10). With all due respect to the latter group, there is a distinct difference between the two sets in terms of club stature. There's a number of reasons that may explain this finding; the loss of European football may cause the chairman of these "big clubs" to invest more, players may be re-motivated having seen their reputations (and possibly pay checks) decreased, and new managers and coaches may be brought in to reinvigorate the squad. All of these may occur to some extent, but there's another factor that probably contributes to a greater degree: regression to the mean[5]. This is a statistical concept that states that when an extreme value occurs (such as Chelsea's and Liverpool's underperformance in 2015/16) it will often naturally move back to the normal value in the next instance. Basically: Chelsea were so bad in 2015/16 that there was no way they could be that bad for a second season in a row!

So it seems then, that the 51.9% of the United Kingdom were right. Well, partially anyway. Europe is bad (if you're going into it anyway), whilst leaving it is...well, maybe good, maybe not, but at least it's far from negative. Teams get worse when going from *out to in*, probably due to the increased number of games resulting in more tiredness, more injuries, and less preparation. Teams get marginally better when going from *in to out*, probably because of regression to the mean.

7. The Big 6-Pointer

The Warm-Up

When it comes to the latter stages of the season, matches between teams engaged in a "relegation battle" are often billed as being "big 6-pointers"[1]. This infers that the outcome of such a game has increased significance compared to other games in determining the fate of the two teams. Unlike the majority of clichés though, there is a theoretical side to this statement. This is because in circumstances where two teams are direct rivals for league position, a single match can potentially provide a 6-point swing. For example, if team A are 2 points ahead of team B, and are about to play them in a match, a win for team A would move them 5 points ahead, whilst a loss would leave them 1 point behind. Therefore the result has a consequential difference of 6 points. Whether or not this theory plays out in the real world of the Premier League is another matter though.

The flip side of this is the idea that the relegation threatened sides have "nothing to lose" when it comes to their matches against the top teams in the league. Despite the lack of evidence supporting both clichés, there have been notable incidents in recent times in which managers have altered their team selections based on these beliefs. For instance, in the 2009/10 season, Wolverhampton Wanderers manager Mick McCarthy made 10 changes to his side for the fixture against Manchester United at Old Trafford, knowing that they had to play Burnley – a fellow relegation struggler – at home five days later[2]. As would probably have been the case regardless of team selection, Wolves lost to Manchester United before then beating Burnley with their more familiar line up. They ended up finishing 15th, 8 points clear of Burnley who were relegated. This is slightly more than the 6-point swing identified earlier, but it still demonstrates the theory nicely.

In the 2017/18 season, newly promoted Newcastle United are scheduled to play title favourites (as of this writing) Manchester City on December 26th. Just four days later they face fellow newcomers Brighton & Hove Albion in what could very well be a "big 6-pointer". Given the congested fixture list (they also play on December 23rd and January 1st), would it be wise for manager Rafa Benitez to follow Mick McCarthy's lead and sacrifice the Manchester City game in order to fully commit to an apparently more important Brighton match? This analysis will look to answer that question.

The Line Ups

The teams finishing in positions 15-20 of the Premier League for each season from 1995/96 to 2015/16 were used in this analysis. These positions were considered to be those in a "relegation battle" and as such, matches between such teams would be classed as "big 6-pointers". To investigate whether "big 6-pointers" were indeed more important than other matches, the analysis will look into whether results against fellow relegation strugglers (RS) managed to predict season outcome ("survived" or "relegated") better than results against mid-table (MT) teams or against title-challenging (TC) teams. Teams finishing in positions 8-12 constituted the mid-table teams whilst teams finishing in positions 1-5 constituted the title-challenging teams. Total points earned in the season against each matchup (RS, MT, and TC) was calculated and compared. Points earned from the return fixture only (i.e. the second time the teams play each during the season) were also analysed (RS2nd, MT2nd, and TC2nd) to see if any effect was greater in "the business end of the season"; another common cliché meaning the latter, more important stage of the season. Survived teams will, in most cases, earn more points than teams which get relegated in each matchup. However, if the cliché is correct, what we should see is that this *difference* is *greater* against RS teams than it is against MT and TC teams.

The Match

The first graph below shows that, as expected, survived teams do indeed gain more points than relegated teams in each matchup across the whole season. To be precise, survived teams average 14.79 points against RS teams, 10.47 points against MT teams, and 5.76 points against TC teams. By contrast, relegated teams average 12.20 points against RS teams, 8.80 points against MT teams, and 4.17 points against TC teams.

The second graph – containing only the data from the return fixtures for each team – shows an *almost* identical picture. Survived teams earn 7.35 points against RS (2nd) teams, 5.24 points against MT (2nd) teams, and 2.91 points against TC (2nd) teams. Relegated teams, on the other hand, earn 6.39 points against RS (2nd) teams, 4.29 points against MT (2nd) teams, and 1.94 points against TC (2nd) teams.

The reason the first and second graphs are only "almost" identical can be seen in the third and final graph. This shows the difference between survived and relegated teams in average points per season in each matchup (RS, MT, and TC teams). When only including data from the return fixtures ("2nd" bars) we see that there is no difference in performance between each matchup. That is, games against RS teams are no more important than games against MT or TC teams. Survived teams do better than relegated teams, but by an almost identical degree in each case. However, when we look at the season as a whole ("All" bars), we find that there is a difference in performance between each matchup. Survived teams again do better than relegated teams in each instance, but now their superiority is greater against RS teams than it is against MT and TC teams. Thus, matches against fellow relegation strugglers – those termed "big 6-pointers" – do seem to have an added importance in determining a team's Premier League fate.

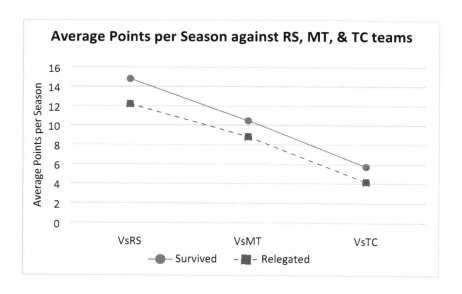

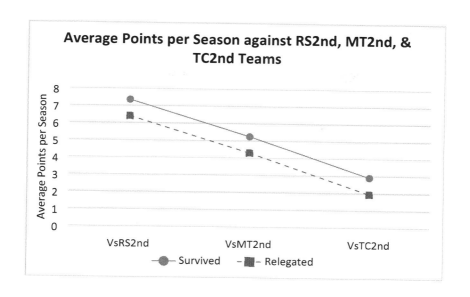

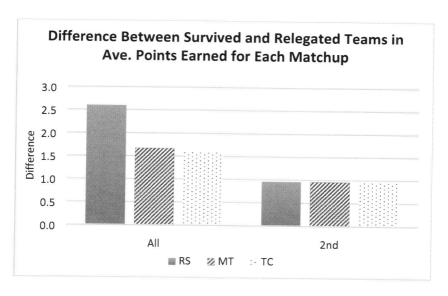

Other Highlights

- Two teams have taken 22 points (from a possible 30) against RS teams – the most points in the analysis. One was Manchester City, who survived in 15th place in the 2005/06 season, and the other was Bolton Wanderers, who were relegated in 18th place in 2011/12. Portsmouth were also relegated having finished bottom in 2009/10, despite gaining 21 points in matches against RS teams, though Sunderland (21 points in 2008/09), Aston Villa (20 in 2005/06), Leeds United (20 in 2002/03) and Southampton (20 in 1999/00) all avoided the drop.

- Of the 19 instances in which a team has achieved less than 10 points against RS teams, 5 survived and 14 were relegated. The lowest of these were Sunderland in 2005/06, who earned 4 points and finished 20th, and Derby County in 2007/08, who earned 5 points and also finished last.

- On only 9 occasions did a team achieve 10 or more points against TC teams; 8 times the team survived. The one team that did get relegated was Sunderland in 1996/97, who earned 11 points by beating Manchester United, Arsenal, and Aston Villa, and drawing against Liverpool and Newcastle United. They finished 18th with 40 points; 1 point from safety. Three teams achieved 12 points (the most in the analysis); West Ham in 2006/07 (15th in the league), Leeds United in 2002/03 (15th), and Everton in 1997/98 (17th).

- 5 teams have managed to come out with 0 points from their 10 fixtures with TC teams (perhaps they were adopting Mick McCarthy's attitude to these matches). Derby County's 2007/08 side – the lowest points scoring team in Premier League history – is, unsurprisingly, one of them. West Bromwich Albion (2008/09) and

Portsmouth (2009/10) both make the list and also finished bottom like Derby. Fulham managed to reach 19th place despite their shut out in points in 2013/14, but most notable of all is the 0 points achieved by Sunderland in the 2007/08 season. They ended the season in 15th place with 39 points, but still couldn't manage even a draw against either Manchester United, Chelsea, Arsenal, Liverpool, or Everton.

- Whilst it wasn't surprising to find that some teams failed in their ability to gain a single point from TC teams, what is perhaps unexpected is the ineptitude of one team to do the same against MT teams. Aston Villa's hopeless 2015/16 side which finished 20th and had the third lowest points total in Premier League history weren't able to grab a solitary point from 10 matches against Liverpool, Stoke City, Chelsea, Everton, and Swansea City.

The Post-Match Interview

The cliché has survived the analysis! Unlike in chapters 3 and 4, where the data dismissed the notion that champions grind out results, and refuted the claims that the Premier League is the most competitive league in the world, here we find that games between relegation battling teams really are more important than other matches. Billing them as "big 6-pointers" is not only accurate in a mathematical sense, but also the metaphorical sense with which they are meant. The fact that the result does not hold when only examining the data from return fixtures is likely to be due to simply having a smaller sample size and a shorter range with which the teams can vary (15 points as opposed to 30).

Does this mean that Mick McCarthy may have been on to something then? To some extent, yes. The prioritisation of RS matches could be a useful strategy given that teams which survive achieve 2.59 more points than teams which get relegated in these games over the course of the season. Given that 2 points or less has separated 17th place from 18th place in 11 of the last 22 seasons, it would seem that the fates of many teams could have been very different had these crucial "big 6-pointers" played out differently. However, McCarthy's willingness to sacrifice his team's fixture against Manchester United – a TC team – may be a little short-sighted. Whilst these matches may not be as important as the "big 6-pointers" against RS teams, the data still shows that survived teams accrue more points in them than do relegated teams. The idea that they have "nothing to lose" is not true. In fact, they have, on average, 5.76 points to lose, whilst relegated teams have 4.17 points to lose. This difference of 1.59 should not be downplayed. Newcastle United (2008/09), Birmingham City (2010/11), and Bolton Wanderers (2011/12) would all have maintained their Premier League status had they picked up an extra point in such games.

8. The Kante Effect

The Warm-Up

Since 2015, perhaps no player has had a greater impact on the Premier League than N'Golo Kante. The French central midfielder arrived at Leicester City on August 3rd a relative unknown quantity. Costing just £7.65 million, he was the 59th most expensive signing of the season (to the Premier League), behind the likes of Abdoulaye Doucoure of Watford, Jordan Veretout of Aston Villa, and Southampton's Jordy Clasie. He cost half of what Everton paid for Oumar Niasse, four times less than what Manchester United paid for Morgan Schneiderlin, and five (!!) times less than what Liverpool paid for Christian Benteke.

72 appearances and 2 Premier League titles later, and N'Golo Kante is now a household name. Countless articles have been written detailing his influence at both Leicester and now Chelsea. Statistics revealing incredible numbers for interceptions, tackling, and distance covered are routinely included[1]. It seems clear that a Kante Effect exists. But have any other players ever had such large impacts when arriving at new clubs?

The Line Ups

Unlike with chapter 11 ('He's Come Back To Haunt Them'), there is no pre-existing categorization of players that is suitable to use when selecting a sample for this analysis. Ultimately, subjective opinion had to be employed. 20 well-known players of the 21st century who it was perceived had made a significant impact to *multiple* football clubs that they had transferred to were identified for data collection (i.e. *not* those who had been developed by the club themselves, or those who had made just one transfer in their career). From this, two values were obtained: an impact on arrival, and an impact on departure. The impact on arrival is calculated by working out the difference in a club's league points total from the season before the player joins, and their first season at the club. The impact on departure is calculated by working out the difference in a club's league points total from the player's final season at the club, and the season after they leave. For each of these, the values are then averaged for all the eligible transfers that the player has been involved in. For example, N'Golo Kante's arrival at Caen led to a 1 point increase, at Leicester a 40 point increase, and at Chelsea, a 43 point increase. This works out at an impact on arrival score of 28 ((1+40+43)/3). A higher positive number for arrival and higher negative number for departure indicate more impactful players (and in a positive fashion).

In order to ensure that one anomalous transfer did not skew the results to an unfair degree, it was decided that that players would only be included if data could be obtained from at least three transfers. For instance, data for N'Golo Kante's impact on arrival can only be taken from his transfers to Caen, Leicester, and Chelsea; a sufficient number for inclusion. His data for impact on departure, however, only includes that from Caen and Leicester, and therefore here he is excluded from the analysis. This left the final analysis consisting of 15 players for the impact on arrival, and 12 players for the impact on departure. Four of the original 20 players identified were not eligible for either impact on arrival or impact on departure. Out of interest, these were Cristiano Ronaldo, Luis Suarez, Mesut Ozil, and Cesc Fabregas; all of which only had eligible data from two transfers for each measure. Further details on the sample and analysis can be found in the 'Specifics of Analyses' chapter.

The Match

First Half: Impact on Arrival

The graph below shows how Kante sits head and shoulders above the 14 other players in his impact on arrival. The 28 point increase he brings to his new team is almost three times higher than the man in second place: Brazil's legendary forward Ronaldo. Like Kante, Ronaldo improved all three of the teams in which data was eligible for his impact on arrival – Barcelona by 10 points, Inter Milan by 10 points, and Real Madrid by 12 points. Zlatan Ibrahimovic rounds up the top three, and his impact should be highlighted for particular praise, given that it is based on data from *seven* different clubs. In fact, every team that the Swede has joined has improved their points tally considerably in his first season, ranging from a 3 point increase at Manchester United, to the 21 point increase at Inter Milan. Interestingly, five players have a negative impact on arrival – meaning that on average, when they join a new team, that team gets worse. Yaya Toure (-0.3 points), Robin van Persie (-2.3), Alexis Sanchez (-2.7), Christian Benteke (-4.5), and Nicolas Anelka (-6.7) make up this enigmatic group. Indeed, Nicolas Anelka has never joined a club that has gone on to improve their points tally in his first season (though it should be noted that despite playing for 12 different clubs during his career, due to data criteria this is based only on his time at Real Madrid, PSG, and Bolton Wanderers). Christian Benteke's low score is largely due to the 18 point decrease that occurred when he transferred from Standard Liege to Genk in 2011 – the highest such decrease in all the data.

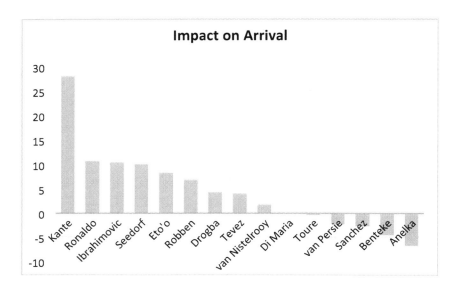

Second Half: Impact on Departure

With Kante's data not eligible (out of interest, based on just two clubs his score was -14.5), it is Didier Drogba who finishes top in the impact on departure. The iconic Chelsea forward has data from five of his past clubs – three of which performed worse when he left. Of these three, the decreases seen by Chelsea (37 points) and Guingamp (24 points) are the first and second biggest in all the data. In 2nd place comes the chronically underrated Samuel Eto'o. The first player to win two proper trebles (domestic league, major domestic cup, and major European cup) has an average impact on departure of -6 points, based on his times at Mallorca, Barcelona, and Inter Milan. Once again Zlatan Ibrahimovic sits in 3rd place, and just to add to his growing legend, he is the only player included in the analysis in which every single team he has left has gone on to perform worse the following season. Again, five players have the ignominious fortune of improving their previous clubs by leaving them. Nicolas Anelka (0.7 points), Christian Benteke (1.3), Edwin van der Sar (3.7), Carlos Tevez (3.8), and Arjen Robben (11.0) make up this list. Robben's departure in particular tends to be a good sign for clubs, with PSV improving by 13 points, Chelsea improving by 2 points, and Real Madrid improving by 18 points.

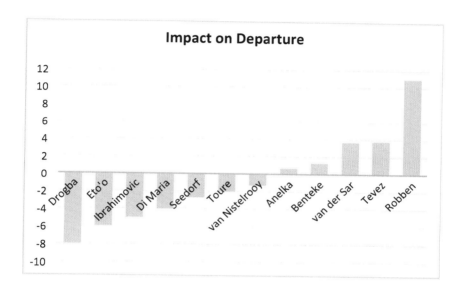

Other Highlights

Some interesting results appeared from the data collection and analysis. Though many of these are not included in the above graphs because they did not fulfil the eligibility requirements, they are still worth taking a quick look at:

- Manchester United's signing of Robin van Persie was hailed by many in the media as the factor that sealed the Premier League title in 2013, but the Dutchman's impact on arrival was exactly 0 points. Edwin van der Sar's transfer seven years earlier was statistically more momentous – with United improving by 6 points that season.

- The departures of Luis Suarez and Gareth Bale from Liverpool and Tottenham Hotspur shared a lot of similarities. Both players were the focal points of attacking minded teams that weren't able win a Premier League title, and both left for one of the La Liga giants – Barcelona and Real Madrid – for huge sums of money. Whilst fans of both clubs clearly missed their talismanic players, Liverpool fans got the worse deal. Suarez's departure led to a massive 22 point decrease for Liverpool, whilst Bale's departure led to just a 3 point decrease for Tottenham.

- As of this writing, two of the biggest transfer stories of the 2017 summer are the possible destinations of Arsenal's star duo, Alexis Sanchez and Mesut Ozil. Where will Arsenal be next season if Sanchez goes? Udinese dropped 2 points when the Chilean left in 2011, but Barcelona actually improved by 7 points in the 2014/15 season. Surprisingly, the potential departure of the much-maligned Mesut Ozil may be more important for Gunners fans. When he left Werder Bremen, the German club went from 61 points to just 41 points, though Real Madrid did improve by 5 points when he left the Bernabeu.

- Finally, whilst his rival may be a one-club man, Cristiano Ronaldo has had his transfers. In his first season at Old Trafford, the greatest/second-greatest (delete as applicable) player of all time oversaw an 8 point decrease. However, Spain was a different story. In his first season there, Ronaldo brought about an 18 point increase for Real Madrid.

The Post-Match Interview

After scoring 28 goals in 46 games in his first season at Manchester United – as well as guiding them to two trophies – it would seem that perceptions of Zlatan Ibrahimovic's greatness is at an all-time high. This analysis should hopefully see that ceiling increase just a little bit further. Ibrahimovic sits 3rd in the impact on arrival and 3rd in the impact on departure, having made every single team he has joined better, and having made every single team he has left worse. This despite having data eligible from more transfers than any other player in the analysis. It is an incredible statistic. Samuel Eto'o also fairs pretty well, coming in fifth (impact on arrival) and second (impact on departure), whilst at the other end of the scale, Nicolas Anelka and Christian Benteke are the only two players who have negative impacts in both measures. Of all the players analysed though, there is one that stands head and shoulders above the rest.

Chelsea signed four players in the summer of 2016, three of which played integral roles in their title triumph (N'Golo Kante, Marcos Alonso, and David Luiz). In addition, a new manager was at the helm in Antonio Conte, so the idea that Kante was the sole reason for their huge improvement should clearly be taken with a pinch of salt. But when it comes on the back of a similarly massive increase with Leicester City, the theory paints a pleasing picture: The Kante Effect. These extraordinary changes in points totals (40 with Leicester and 43 with Chelsea) should not be understated. Such an improvement for Stoke City could have led them to be champions in 2017 (is this any less realistic than Leicester's achievement?), or alternatively, could have resulted in Crystal Palace qualifying for the Champions League. One thing is for sure, it'll be interesting to see the impact of Kante's next transfer, both on Chelsea, and on the prospective club.

.

9. The Value of a Cup Run

The Warm Up

In the 2016/17 season, Everton, West Bromwich Albion, AFC Bournemouth, and Stoke City were knocked out of the F.A. Cup third round. The latter three eliminated by lower division clubs. At the time, these teams sat 7th, 8th, 9th, and 11th in the Premier League. Firmly mid-table, with no real chance of going higher (Manchester United in 6th were already 9 points clear at that point) and no real chance of getting relegated (they all survived by at least 10 points). In such circumstances, you would think that an F.A. Cup run would be the primary target for the remainder of the season. With the big boys fighting amongst themselves for titles and champions league positions, the F.A. Cup offered these clubs – and their fans – a chance at of a trophy (or at least a day out at Wembley!) and an alternative path to Europe for next season. Yet when these teams took to the pitch for what should have been the start of a magical F.A. Cup journey, Everton had rested three players (fair enough), Stoke City had rested four players (a little questionable), West Bromwich Albion had rested five players (okay now that seems odd), and Bournemouth had rested 10 – yes 10! – of their usual line up. The decision seemed strange at the time...90 minutes later having lost 3-0 to a League One team in Millwall it seemed downright foolish and disrespectful.

The concept of resting players in the F.A. Cup is relatively new. A quick bit of research on Google suggests that it didn't become commonplace until probably the mid-2000s; prior to this, the practice was reserved only for its younger and less glamorous sibling – the league cup. Even in its early days, it tended to only be the big teams that employed it, indeed, it was probably only the likes of Arsenal, Manchester United, Chelsea, and Liverpool who had squads deep enough that they could afford to. But as the money coming into the Premier League continued to rise, so did the importance of staying in it. And as a consequence, the priority of the F.A. Cup seems to have lessened. Nowadays it is not uncommon to see *any* team – whatever level – resting players when it comes to the cup. Premier League relegation battlers are desperate to stay up, Championship teams are striving for promotion, and even League One teams know that in theory they could be in the promised land in less than two years. Why throw these opportunities away when in all likelihood one of the big teams is going to win it anyway (Wigan Athletic and Portsmouth being the only exceptions in the past 22 seasons)?

Decisions like Eddie Howe's then are perhaps not an intentional disdain for the cup per se, but rather a simple indication of priorities. Even if Bournemouth weren't in any danger of going down, the difference between each final league position was £2 million in 2016/17. Despite the mind-boggling finances currently in football, this amount still talks; especially to the chairman of the clubs. Just two points separated Southampton in 8th and Stoke City in 13th that season; one win for Mark Hughes men would have equated to £10 million. By contrast, winning the F.A. Cup earned Arsenal £1.8 million. Now it's getting easier to see why squads get rotated. A day out at Wembley would be great, but ensuring the best players are fit for important league fixtures either side of these matches are of greater concern. But is this indifference warranted? Is a cup run really detrimental to league performance? Or could it possibly even be beneficial?

The Line Ups

The league performance of Premier League teams will be compared before F.A. Cup elimination and after F.A. Cup elimination. This will then be broken down into those eliminated at the 3rd round, 4th round, 5th round, and quarter finals. Those reaching the semi final stages will not be included in the analysis as the number of games following this point is too small to warrant a decent sized sample for league performance. If a cup run is *detrimental* to league performance, we should see a large, negative change in points per game for those eliminated in the quarter finals and a large, positive change in points per game for those eliminated in the 3rd round. Likewise, if a cup run is *beneficial* to league performance, we should see a large, positive change in points per game for those eliminated in the quarter finals and a large, negative change in points per game for those eliminated in the 3rd round. Data has been taken from each season between 1997/98 and 2016/17. For instances in which an F.A. Cup match went to a replay, the points before and points after data are based on the date of the replay, not the initial match.

Additionally, it was decided to compare the number of 'increasers' (teams that improved their league performance following their exit from the F.A. Cup) with the number of 'decreasers' (teams that declined in league performance following their exit from the F.A. Cup elimination) for each round of elimination.

The Match

First Half: Change in Points

Over the past 20 years, 112 Premier League teams have been eliminated from the F.A. Cup in 3rd round, 104 in the 4th round, 65 in the 5th round, and 54 in the quarter finals. From these 334 data points, the graph below shows that an F.A. Cup run has pretty much no influence whatsoever on league performance. Regardless of the round that a team is eliminated, the team will continue to perform as they had done previously. Indeed, for the 3rd and 5th round, the change is exactly 0. The largest change – a 0.09 decrease in league performance following elimination at the quarter final stage – would equate to less than 1 point based on teams only playing an average of 9.7 league matches after this point. Two things may be at work here: either cup progression is genuinely having no effect on league matches, or the negatives of a cup run (increased tiredness, potential injuries, etc.) are balanced equally with the positives of a cup run (increased confidence, motivation, etc.).

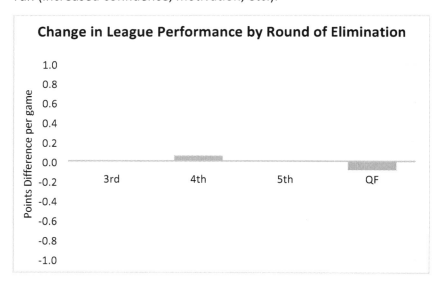

Second Half: Increasers and Decreasers

Based on the above graph, you would perhaps expect the number of increasers and decreasers to be fairly similar for each round, but surprisingly that is not the case, at least not for the 3rd round. Despite an average change in points per game of exactly 0, there were 16 fewer teams which improved following 3rd round elimination than those which declined. Exploring this further, we see that the average increase (+0.36) is considerably greater than the average decrease (-0.27) for these teams. Whilst this doesn't seem like much, given that teams tend to play around 17-18 league games following an exit in the 3rd round, an improvement of 0.36 points per game equates to a sizeable 6.3 point gain. For the decreasers, this decline of 0.27 points per game equates to a substantial 4.7 point loss. It seems that the majority of teams that get eliminated in the 3rd round go on to get worse, but of the teams that do get better, they get better to a considerable degree.

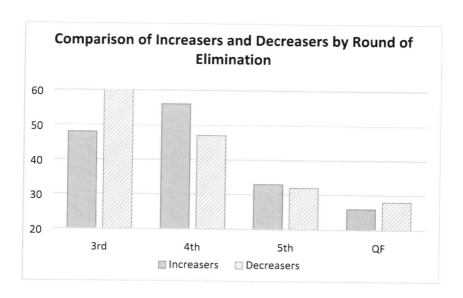

Other Highlights

- The biggest decline in league performance following a 3rd round exit was by the 2013/14 Newcastle United team. Prior to being knocked out by Cardiff City, the Magpies sat in 8th place in the Premier League, averaging 1.65 points per game. They went on to lose 12 of their remaining 18 games, averaging just 0.89 points per game. Had they done this from the start of the season, they would have finished on 34 points – 1 point and 1 place outside the relegation zone.

- The biggest improvement in league performance following a 3rd round exit was by the 2015/16 Southampton team. Before being eliminated by Crystal Palace, the Saints had taken a respectable 24 points from their first 20 games. Remarkably, they then went on to win 12 of their remaining 18, averaging 2.17 points per game. The good form took them from 13th to 6th, but had they done this from the start, they'd have actually ended up beating Leicester City to the title by 1 point.

- Speaking of which, the 2000/01 Leicester City side have the ignominious record of performing worst after an F.A. Cup quarter final defeat. The foxes surprise elimination at the hands of Wycombe Wanderers sparked a run of 8 successive losses, and 9 defeats in their final 10 games. The unprecedented collapse saw them go from 4th place to 13th.

- By contrast, exiting at the quarter final stage ended up being a good thing for the 2005/06 Newcastle United team. After losing to Chelsea on March 22nd, they went on to win 6 and draw 1 of their final 8 games. The run helped lift them from 12th to 7th and included the scalps of Tottenham Hotspur, arch-rivals Sunderland, and Chelsea.

The Post-Match Interview

In 2013 Wigan Athletic won their one and only F.A. Cup, defeating Manchester City in the final. Yet they could only muster 36 points in the league, and were relegated in 18th place. This, in itself, may provide evidence for the relegation battling managers who argue their case when fielding weakened teams, but it is strengthened even more when you consider Wigan's previous season. In 2011/12 the club were sitting 18th in the league, with only 15 points from 20 games. They were then knocked out of the F.A. Cup 3rd round by Swindon Town but responded by taking 28 points from their final 18 matches; finishing 15th in the league and surviving relegation against all odds. Was this revival due to fitter players no longer having to take part in tiresome F.A. Cup matches? Would the 2012/13 team have done the same had they been knocked out by Bournemouth in the third round, instead of winning 1-0 in a replay? We'll obviously never know, and whilst it is a tempting conclusion to make, the analyses here wouldn't really support it.

When you take only the change in points data, it looks like there's no impact whatsoever of a cup run (or lack of) on league performance. Even the biggest change (occurring when eliminated at the quarter final stage) equates to less than one point, whilst no change *at all* is found when exiting at the 3rd and 5th rounds. The second analysis confuses things slightly though, with there being a considerable difference in increasers (teams improving post-exit) and decreasers (teams declining post-exit). Just 43% of teams that get knocked out in the 3rd round go on to improve their points per game, but they tend to do so to a large degree: 6.3 points on average.

This is a difficult finding to explain, and it could well be that it is merely an *ignis fatuus* of the data. If it's not, then one possible idea is that it relates to a famous saying that *may* apply in Premier League football: "the cream always rises to the top". That is, the better teams improve as the season goes on. As a net consequence of this assumption, poorer teams must get worse as the season goes on. Support for this comes from data that shows – unsurprisingly – that teams that get knocked out of the F.A. Cup 3rd round tend to be not as good as the teams that progress. Over the past 20 years, the average final league position of Premier League teams eliminated in the 3rd round is 12.4, the 4th round; 11.2, 5th round; 9.8, quarter finals; 10.4, and semi finals; 7.0. Thus, the *majority* of teams eliminated in the 3rd round are poorer teams who may "naturally" get worse as the season progresses; though there may be the occasional good team eliminated who improve. By contrast, teams eliminated in the 5th round and quarter finals are of more similar ability, and therefore there is random (and therefore likely equal) chance of both increases and decreases in performance. This theory would fit with the results of the two analyses conducted, and could easily be tested in a future analysis...perhaps in "The Inner Geek in Football 2"...

10. The League of Extraordinary Managers

The Warm-Up

La Liga may have Messi, Ronaldo, Bale, and Neymar, but when it comes to the top managers, the Premier League is king. The top six are all led by names revered around the footballing world. Arsenal have Arsene Wenger: winner of three Premier League titles, seven F.A. Cups (the most ever), and a man who – if he sees out his contract – will have managed more Premier League matches than anyone in the history of the game. North London rivals Tottenham Hotspur have Mauricio Pochettino: a man who guided the club to their highest league position in 54 years and who has been linked in the past with the likes of Barcelona and Manchester United[1,2]. Liverpool have Jurgen Klopp: a charismatic figure who led previous club Borussia Dortmund to back-to-back Bundesliga titles en route to becoming their longest serving manager. Chelsea have Antonio Conte: winner of three successive Serie A titles with Juventus – one of which was an unbeaten season – and of course, the man who brought the title back to Stamford Bridge in 2016/17. Manchester City have Pep Guardiola: a man whose philosophy on football strategy is so admired that it *almost* overshadows the three La Liga titles, three Bundesliga titles, and two Champions Leagues that he has managed to win in just eight seasons of management. And last but certainly not least, Manchester United have Jose Mourinho: the only man able to rival Guardiola's trophy cabinet. He has won eight league titles in four different countries, won the Champions league twice and the Europa League/UEFA cup twice, and won eight domestic cups. He also led Chelsea and Real Madrid to the highest points totals ever recorded in the Premier League and La Liga, respectively, and between February 2002 and April 2011 went 150 league matches at home unbeaten.

It would be hard for anyone to argue that this is not the greatest collection of managers in one league at the same time ever. Who, though – to use a phrase coined by Mr Mourinho himself – really is the Special One? It's a great debate to have, and one that's likely influenced by subjective factors such as playing style and personality, or an individual's preferences for cup wins and the blooding of youngsters. But can we find an objective measure by analysing real data and statistics? One way may be through examining the impact they have in terms of league points when arriving and departing a club.

The Line Ups

In most situations, the league is the priority for a club and a manager, so this analysis will focus only on this aspect. A very similar method will be used as in chapter 8 ('The Kante Effect'). To measure impact, the average points total a manager achieves with a club will be calculated from each *full* season they completed there. For example, in the seven seasons that Klopp was in charge at Dortmund, they achieved 59, 57, 75, 81, 66, 71, and 46 points, which averages at 64.9 points. This value is then compared with the points the club scored in the one *full* season before arrival ('impact on arrival') and the points the club scored in the one *full* season after departure ('impact on departure'). Dortmund scored 40 points in the season prior to Klopp and 78 points in the season post-Klopp, thus Klopp's impact on arrival at Dortmund would be 24.9 points (64.9 – 40) and impact on departure 13.1 points (78 – 64.9). This process is then repeated and averaged for all the other clubs that the manager has managed at least one *full* season with. Therefore in Klopp's case, this would be Bundesliga side FSV Mainz 05, and Liverpool, though with the latter, only the 'impact on arrival' is applicable given his continued leadership of the Merseyside club.

The Match

First Half: Impact on Arrival

The data shows that Conte has a *huge* impact on his arrival at a club — adding almost twice as many points as the next best manager, Jurgen Klopp. At Bari they improved from 50 to 80 points, at Juventus from 58 to 91, and at Chelsea from 50 to 93. These are phenomenal increases; over 12(!!) additional wins per season on average. The sort of number that not only would have kept Sunderland in the Premier League in 2016/17, but would have had them competing for a European place too. Klopp's data is also taken from three clubs: FSV Mainz 05 (14.5 point increase), Borussia Dortmund (24.9 point increase), and Liverpool (14 point increase). Arsene Wenger is third, marginally ahead of Pep Guardiola. Wenger's Arsenal team average 75.6 points in the league, compared to this 63 they achieved in the full season prior to his arrival ("Wenger-Outers" take note!). The Frenchman also improved Nancy and Monaco by 1.7 and 6.7 points respectively. Guardiola took over Barcelona after they had attained 67 points in La Liga, and in his four seasons there they yielded an impressive 93.1 points. And whilst his average at Bayern Munich was even higher still (85.7 — but over a 38 game season this equates to 95.8), he arrived on the back of Jupp Heynckes incredible treble-winning side that won the league with 91 points. Despite what was widely considered a disappointing first season in charge at Manchester City,

Guardiola did achieve 12 more points than in the previous campaign under Manuel Pellegrini. In 5th place is Jose Mourinho, the only manager to have data taken from more than three clubs. He improved Porto and Chelsea before overseeing slight decreases in league points with Inter Milan and Real Madrid (despite winning the treble with the former in 2009/10). Since his return to England he has improved both Chelsea (see 'Specifics of the Analyses' chapter for the obvious caveat here) and Manchester United. Finally, Mauricio Pochettino comes in last. His impact on arrival is based on only two clubs due to Southampton having played in the Championship in the season before his arrival. Under his leadership, Espanyol declined by 1.6 points, though Tottenham Hotspur have improved by 4.3 points.

Interestingly the top 3 managers here (Conte, Klopp, and Wenger) have never failed to improve one of the clubs that they have moved to, whilst the bottom 3 managers (Guardiola, Mourinho, and Pochettino) all have on at least one occasion. It is quite fitting (and fortunate for the reputation-builders of such managers – like myself) that all managers do average a *positive* number. That is, on their arrival at a club, they tend to increase the amount of league points achieved.

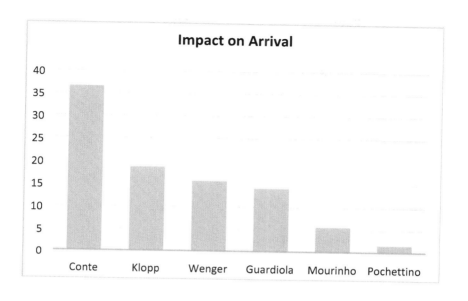

Impact on Arrival

Second Half: Impact on Departure

Whilst there are limitations with the impact on arrival data, the general idea is based on reasonably sound logic: the better a manager is, the more a team should improve their league performance when he arrives. The logic for the impact on departure results are not so simple. I would argue that the worse a team performs after a manager leaves, the better that manager must be. Without him, they decline. However, it could be argued that in fact, the opposite is true. If a manger leaves a club and their league performances deteriorates, it is because he has "left a mess behind", so to speak.

For example, Guardiola averaged 93.1 points at Barcelona, but in the season after he resigned, they scored 100 points. This could mean two things depending on how you look at it, either a) Guardiola is a good manager because it was he that put the foundations in place for the club to continue to be successful, and he has essentially left a legacy behind, or b) Guardiola is not that good a manager, because on his departure the club improved – implying that maybe anybody could have done what he did (if not more). The reverse has the same issue. Mourinho averaged 92.3 points at Real Madrid, and in the season after he left, they scored only 87. Does that mean that he is a good manager because when he was gone, the club got worse? Or a bad one because it was he that allowed the club to come to turmoil before leaving? As mentioned above, I will be opting for the first approach when describing the subsequent graphs. Declines in league performance (indicated by negative values in the data) suggest a *good* manager. Feel free, though, to interpret them however you feel!

Jose Mourinho now leads the way, though Antonio Conte again performs well, finishing in second. These are the only two managers whose teams tend to perform worse after they have departed. In particular, of the five eligible teams included in Mourinho's data, it is only Chelsea (after his second spell) that went on to improve after he left. Porto decreased by 19.9 points, Chelsea (first time) by 6.7, Inter Milan by 6.8, and Real Madrid by 5.3. Conte and Arsene Wenger – second and third – are based only on their times at Juventus and Monaco, respectively. The Italian club achieved 3.8 fewer points the season after Conte left, whilst the French club achieved 1.1 more after Wenger left. Pep Guardiola again places just below Wenger in fourth. The Barcelona side he left improved by 6.9 points though the Bayern Munich side he left performed worse by 3.7 points. Mauricio Pochettino resides in 5th; his Espanyol side got worse (4.4 point decrease) but his Southampton side got better (4.0 point increase) after he left each. Were he to make a shock exit before the 2017/18 season, Tottenham should – based on this average – finish with 88 points; a total that would win the Premier League title 59% of the time over the last 22 seasons. Finally, Jurgen Klopp, second in the impact on arrival, now finishes last – by a considerable margin – in the impact on departure. As with Guardiola and Pochettino, this is based on only two clubs, though the improvements each made in the season after he left them were considerable. FSV Mainz 05 went from averaging 59.5 points to scoring 63, whilst Borussia Dortmund went from averaging 64.9 points to scoring 78.

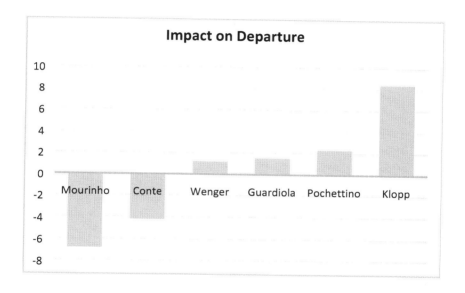

Extra Time: Total Impact

Given the ambiguity in interpreting the impact on departure results, it makes any attempt to create a 'total impact' graph very difficult for the same reasons already discussed. Nevertheless, I will give it a go. The graph below is produced by flipping the impact on departure values such that minus numbers become positive ones (and vice versa) and then subtracting these from the impact on arrival values. Thus, Conte's total impact is 36.48 + 4.18 = 40.66. Again, this represents my personal opinion that takes the view that decreases in points following departure indicates a good manager, and increases in points following departure indicate a not-so-good manager. As such, if you share this opinion, the graph below presents a nice, final take on who really is the best manager in the Premier League, and if you don't...well, you're welcome to ignore it!

So Antonio Conte takes home the gold, miles ahead of his rivals. The Chelsea manager finished first in impact on arrival and second in impact on departure, so it's no surprise that his total impact score was almost three times greater than the next manager. Arsene Wenger – for all his detractors – came in second, with his consistent performances in both arrival and departure contributing to this. Amazingly, the managers of both Manchester clubs – rivals Pep Guardiola and Jose Mourinho – finished on *exactly the same* score...even when going down to two decimal places. Given the possible variations within the data this is an incredible coincidence, and, perhaps annoyingly to some, means that this article is sitting squarely on the fence in the debate over who is better: the Master of Tiki Taka, or the Special One. Coming in 5th is media favourite Jurgen Klopp, whose poor impact on departure score means the Liverpool man's total impact is only 10.3. Finally, bringing up the rear is Tottenham's Mauricio Pochettino. He is arguably the least revered, globally, of the six (which says more about the high regard that the other five are held in, rather than his own reputation), and so perhaps it is no surprise that his total impact is the lowest. He is, though, the youngest of all the managers, and another good season at Tottenham – say, an 80 point haul – would put him right on Mourinho's coattails in the impact on arrival table, and turn his marginally negative total impact into a positive one.

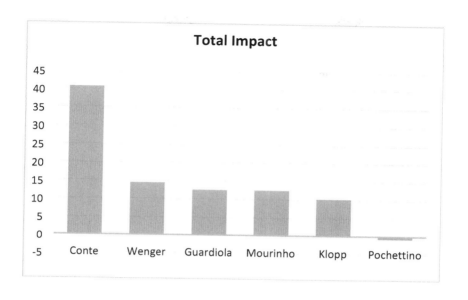

The Post-Match Interview

If we stick to the less-contentious impact on arrival data, we see that Antonio Conte is the clear leader, whilst Mauricio Pochettino is in last place. The ambiguous impact on departure and total impact results don't actually change things *too* much, with the only major movement being with Mourinho (upwards) and Klopp (downwards).

So who is the Special One? In a league that boasts six managers with a combined 24 major league titles, 21 domestic cups, and 6 major European triumphs, Antonio Conte (probably) comes out on top. Which is apt considering that, as of this writing, he is the current Premier League champion, having guided last season's 10th placed Chelsea team to the title with the second highest points total ever achieved. As with Chapter 1's 'Too Big To Go Down' analysis, the judgement of best manager is, ultimately, a subjective one. Whether it is possible to factor in values for trophies won or attractiveness of playing style is a challenge from a later date, though it is interesting because if it were possible to account for these, there would no doubt be two main beneficiaries. The two managers who are arguably *perceived* as the best in the world by the media, fans, and players alike. The two managers currently overseeing things at the Manchester giants. The two managers who scored exactly the same for total impact. The two managers being Jose Mourinho and Pep Guardiola.

11. He's Come Back to Haunt Them

The Warm-Up

"Frank Lampard close to tears and lost for words after scoring the equaliser he didn't expect for Manchester City against Chelsea." (Daily Mail Online Headline: September 21st, 2014)[1].

All Chelsea fans will remember it. Most football fans probably do too. After scoring 147 Premier League goals for Chelsea, the legendary midfielder had come back to haunt his old club. It was always going to happen. And yet whilst this is memorable, it's certainly not the most famous instance of such an occurrence. Back in 1974, Manchester United great Denis Law – scorer of 237 goals in 404 appearances for the Red Devils – was now plying his trade for the blue side of Manchester. When the two teams met on the 27th of April, a win for City over their arch-rivals would result in United being relegated to the second tier of English football for the first time since 1937. What would happen? Of course City won. And of course Law scored the only goal of the game.

These things seem to happen all the time; far more than they should. Even if we don't notice it ourselves initially, we will no doubt be told it by the commentator, or the news reporter. In the first half of the 2016/17 season alone, we saw Cesc Fabregas score against Arsenal, Shane Long bag against West Brom, Younes Kaboul net against Tottenham, and both Wilfried Bony and Andre Ayew get on the scoresheet for different clubs against Swansea. But whilst it seems like these are regular occurrences, is that actually the case? Does the data back it up?

The Line Ups

The first thing to remember in this analysis is that when the phrase "he's come back to haunt them" is used in football, it refers only to instances in which a player has scored against a previous club *after* having left them. It does not include instances when a player scores against a previous club *prior* to joining them. Whilst this may seem obvious, it is important to remember when analysing the data. For example, Jimmy Floyd Hasselbaink's overall record against Chelsea is 3 goals in 10 games, but his record against Chelsea whilst playing for Middlesbrough/Charlton Athletic/Cardiff City (i.e. *after* leaving them) is 1 in 6. It is this second piece of data that is used in the analysis.

It could be argued that simply calculating the goals-to-game ratio of a player against his previous club would provide a sufficient account of whether he has "come back to haunt them". However, this misses a key factor: expected ability. For instance, Alan Shearer's 10 goals in 15 games against Blackburn Rovers (0.67 ratio) is superior to Emile Heskey's 3 goals in 7 games against Leicester City (0.43). However, Shearer was a much more prolific goal scorer – so we should expect this. A better analysis of whether a player has come back to haunt his old team should account for this by comparing it to a player's career goals-to-game ratio. By subtracting the overall career ratio (Shearer's was 0.59) from the team-specific ratio (0.67 for Shearer against Blackburn), we are left with a *ratio difference*. The higher the ratio difference, the more a player came back to haunt his old team. A negative ratio difference suggests that the player actually performed below expectations when facing his old club.

The next step is identifying a sample. Clearly, there are countless players that have returned to score (let alone simply played) against an ex-club; it would be an impossible task to examine them all. This analysis has chosen to focus only on an elite group: those of the Premier League 100 club. Of these 26 players, only those that have scored Premier League goals for multiple teams can be included, and as such 7 are excluded*. The ratio difference was calculated for the remaining 19 players for each club that they scored a Premier League goal for and subsequently left. That is, for Jermain Defoe, his ratio difference against West Ham United, Tottenham Hotspur, and Portsmouth was calculated, but not against AFC Bournemouth, Toronto, or Sunderland.

From this we are left with 67 "pieces" of data. However, there are numerous instances in which players only faced a previous club on a few occasions. Such small sample sizes would unfairly skew the results. For example, Robin van Persie scored 1 goal in 1 appearance against Manchester United, whilst Robbie Keane scored 3 goals in 3 appearances against Leeds United. These 1.00 ratios may not accurately represent performance; basically, the players may have just gotten lucky in those games (or unlucky if the ratio was really low). To account for this, only instances in which a player faced his old club a minimum of 5 times were included. This resulted in a final sample size of 35 instances across 17 players.

Out of interest these are Matthew Le Tissier, Didier Drogba, Paul Scholes, Ryan Giggs, Sergio Aguero, Steven Gerrard, and Thierry Henry.

The Match

The graph below shows the ratio differences for all 35 instances. The key for each number can be found in chapter 13's 'Specifics of the Analyses', but the important point to note from this is the actual picture presented. Far more players *do not* come back to haunt their old team than ones that do. Of the 35 instances, only 12 had a positive ratio difference – and only 1 of these was higher than +0.10. By contrast, of the 23 that had a negative ratio difference (i.e., the player performed worse than normal when playing his old club) 17 were lower than -0.10.

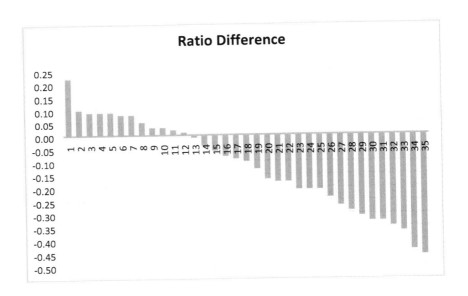

The next graph is simply a filtered version of the previous one. Whereas the previous version often contained multiple instances from the same player (e.g., there are five for Peter Crouch), the below graphs shows only *one* instance per player. This one instance is from the team that the player is most associated with, based on appearances and/or goals for said club. So in Peter Crouch's case, his ratio difference against Liverpool is shown as this is his ex-club where he played and scored most. Again, the same pattern emerges, with 5 players "coming back to haunt" their old team, and 12 not. It is also probably not surprising that players are more likely to "come back to haunt" their old team if that team is a "small" club (no disrespect to Leicester, Blackburn, Coventry, and West Ham) as opposed to a "big" club (e.g. Chelsea, Manchester United, and Liverpool).

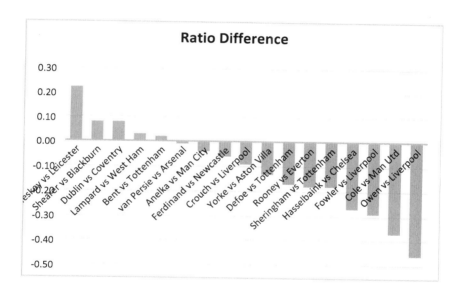

Other Highlights

- Nicolas Anelka has "come back to haunt" all 4 of his eligible ex-clubs (i.e. those in which the data is sufficient for analysis). He scored 7 against Arsenal, 5 against Liverpool, and 3 a piece against Manchester City and

Bolton Wanderers. This total of 18 goals is the highest amongst all the players included in the full analysis.

- Second to Anelka in the goals-versus-old-clubs charts is Peter Crouch with 14. It took him 64 matches to achieve that tally though – the most number of appearances against ex-clubs of all the players included in the full analysis.

- Dwight Yorke, Andrew Cole, and Teddy Sheringham were 3 of Manchester United's famous front line in their historic treble campaign of 1999. But how did they all fare once they left the Red Devils? In a combined 32 appearances against United, they managed just 1 goal – and that was by Cole in a 3-1 league cup tie defeat for Blackburn Rovers. It's safe to say none of them came back to haunt Sir Alex Ferguson.

The Post-Match Interview

Looking at the graphs, these may not seem like big differences, but to put them in perspective, let's take a look at the top two Premier League goal scorers of all time. If every game Alan Shearer had played had been against Blackburn Rovers, he'd have ended up with 295 Premier League goals, rather than 260. And if every game Wayne Rooney had played had been against Everton, he'd be on 113 Premier League goals instead of 198. These small differences (+0.08 for Shearer and -0.18 for Rooney) may not seem like much, but they would have a big impact over a whole career.

However, regardless of the magnitude, this analysis clearly shows one thing: players do *not* come back to haunt their old teams as often as you would believe (or at least are told!). This makes sense too. If the same manager and players are still there from when the player was at the club, all of his strengths and weaknesses are known to the opposition, meaning goal-scoring may be a little trickier than normal (this certainly may explain the Yorke/Cole/Sheringham statistic given that Sir Alex Ferguson resided over Manchester United long after they all left). The not-so-endearing reaction of ex-fans may also explain these results. When Wayne Rooney returns to Goodison Park, he doesn't exactly get a hero's welcome, and thus, it is completely possible that this negatively affects his performances against them. Of course, it could be argued that these strikers also know the weaknesses of the opposing defenders, and that the hostile environment may actually motivate them to excel under such conditions, but that doesn't fit as nicely with the data.

What is probably happening here are two cognitive phenomenon called the availability heuristic and confirmation bias. The availability heuristic suggests that we overestimate the likelihood of an event happening (e.g., a player scoring against their old club) because of how unusual or emotionally charged that event may be (Frank Lampard's goal for Manchester City against Chelsea would certainly constitute the latter)[2]. Confirmation bias (the remembering of information that endorses our preconceptions) then cements these views further[3]. You don't remember all the times that Romelu Lukaku *didn't* score against Chelsea. Or all those occasions when Andy Carroll drew a blank against Liverpool. Or the matches when Daniel Sturridge failed to find the net against Manchester City. You don't remember them because they are not memorable, and because they don't confirm our preconceptions.

12. End of Season Review

The players have put their shifts in, they've got their passports in hand, and they're ready to put their feet up on the beach in some exotic (and expensive) location. Or as is the case now in the ever-lasting cycle of football: go on international duty to play in tedious qualifiers, meaningless friendlies, and pointless tournaments (here's looking at you, Confederations Cup). Nevertheless, before we call time on the *real* football season, there's one last event in the calendar: the End of Season Review. A time to heap adulation on the deserved, honourably mention the hard-working, and have a "friendly" little dig at the ones that need a kick up the backside.

By my reckoning, Real World Data United defeated Conventional Wisdom City 3-2. Chapters 3, 4, and 11 provided solid evidence that champions do not have a superior ability to grind out results, the English Premier League isn't the most competitive in the world, and forwards are more likely to struggle against their former teams rather than come back to haunt them. Yet it wasn't all bad news for cliché enthusiasts. We found that leaving Europe does indeed bring about a benefit in league performance, whilst big 6-pointers really are of heightened importance to relegation battlers. Playing Devil's advocate can often be a fun thing to do, and perhaps no more so than in football. These iconoclastic findings will hopefully allow you to speak up confidently the next time you're sitting in the pub and a friend proclaims that Arsenal's 1-0 win over

Burnley is a good sign for the Gunners. Or that Mohamed Salah's goal against Chelsea was inevitable.

Elsewhere it was revealed that the 2016 Aston Villa team were the biggest to ever get relegated from the Premier League, and that based on this, only six of the current lot (2017/18) are "too big to go down"...none of which are named Manchester City. Strong cases were made to justify the huge sums of money spent on John Stones and Raheem Sterling over the past two years...cases that may look even better by the end of summer 2017 if any of the Kylian Mbappe, Alexis Sanchez, Alexandre Lacazette, or Cristiano Ronaldo rumours come true. Speaking of whom, it could be argued that the Real Madrid icon is the reason that Wayne Rooney doesn't receive the love that someone who is Manchester United and England's greatest ever goal-scorer should probably be entitled to. Two players that do get their fair share of praise are N'Golo Kante and Zlatan Ibrahimovic, and it was shown that when it comes to making an impact at a club, nobody does it better than these. When it comes to the F.A. Cup, it may have lost some of its magic but a good run doesn't seem to negatively affect league performance...granted, nor does it seem to have a positive effect either, but still, let's hope the results encourage some managers to field full strength sides. And finally, when attempting to settle the argument of who the Premier League's top man is, the data couldn't split the two giants of Mourinho and Guardiola...but did suggest someone even better: the man who has won the league title in his last four seasons in club management, Antonio Conte.

To repeat what was hopefully emphasised strongly at the start of this book and throughout: these analyses are *not* water-tight answers to football's biggest questions. They are just an attempt to remove the subjectivity from a debate and replace it with real-world, objective data. Some chapters are more limited than others (the small sample sizes within 'The Kante Effect' and 'The League of Extraordinary Managers' are a particular drawback) but all, I hope, are fresh in the methods they use.

Football as a game is simple. It involves kicking a ball into a goal. Football as a competition is complicated. It involves transfers of varying amounts, managerial reigns of unpredictable lengths, changes in league status, fluctuations in a player, coach, or chairman's prioritises, and many, many more factors. Critics of sports analytics often say that number-crunching takes the beauty out of sport by reducing complex and interesting phenomenon into simple and measurable pieces, but I think that this book demonstrates that the truth is quite the opposite. In most cases, an analysis opens up as many new questions as it answers; surely a good thing for the fan worried that Google may soon be capable of replacing all pub-based debate. The French Ligue 1 is the most competitive league in the world...but is there a way to measure entertainment too? Or quality? And if so, could you combine all three to come up with an overall "Best League in the World?"

Being aware of what real data says allows you to add another perspective but it doesn't mean you have to replace a pre-existing one. Stats geeks can have subjective opinions and opponents of stats can use numbers too. I think the idea that there are two mutually exclusive sides is mostly in the past already, but we still have some way to go before the casual football conversation contains caveats rather than clichés. There's a famous saying that is often paraphrased as follows:

"There are three kinds of lies: lies, damned lies, and statistics"

This could not be further from the truth. Statistics are a gold standard. You just have to be aware of where they come from.

13.Specifics of the Analyses

i.   Too Big To Go Down

- A full table of all 76 teams who have been relegated from the Premier League, plus the 2018 teams (green) and other notable cases (red):

Rank	Team	Year	Score
	Manchester United	2018	4456
	Arsenal	2018	5025
	Liverpool	2018	5152
	Chelsea	2018	9918
	Tottenham Hotspur	2018	10143
	Chelsea	2016	10453
	Everton	1998	11485
	Everton	2018	11652
	Tottenham Hotspur	2004	12025
1	Aston Villa	2016	14335
2	Leeds United	2004	15705
	Manchester City	2018	16487
3	Nottingham Forest	1997	16599
4	Nottingham Forest	1999	16911
5	Newcastle United	2016	17591
6	Nottingham Forest	1993	17624
	Newcastle United	2018	18070
7	Newcastle United	2009	18209
8	Manchester City	1996	18351
	West Ham United	2018	18411
9	West Ham United	2003	18517
10	Southampton	2005	18524

11	West Ham United	2011	18929
	Leeds United	1993	20406
12	Coventry City	2001	22234
13	Manchester City	2001	22776
	Southampton	2018	23096
14	Ipswich Town	2002	23339
15	Ipswich Town	1995	24397
16	Leicester City	2002	25260
17	Leicester City	2004	25425
18	Blackburn Rovers	2012	25548
19	Sheffield Wednesday	2000	25975
20	Middlesbrough	2009	26041
21	Sunderland	2017	26729
22	Norwich City	1995	27657
23	Middlesbrough	2017	27741
24	Queens Park Rangers	1996	27776
25	Leicester City	1995	27829
26	Derby County	2002	27989
27	Norwich City	2005	28090
	West Bromwich Albion	2018	28976
28	Norwich City	2016	29432
29	Derby County	2008	29634
30	Norwich City	2014	29699
	Leicester City	2018	29703
	Leicester City	2017	30248
31	Sunderland	2006	31141
32	Sunderland	2003	31717
33	Queens Park Rangers	2015	32733
34	West Bromwich Albion	2006	32740
35	West Bromwich Albion	2009	32771
36	Blackburn Rovers	1999	32776
37	West Bromwich Albion	2003	32873
38	Birmingham City	2011	32910
39	Queens Park Rangers	2013	33021
	Crystal Palace	2018	33126
	Stoke City	2018	33471
40	Middlesbrough	1997	33646

41	Wolverhampton Wanderers	2012	33661
42	Wolverhampton Wanderers	2004	33715
43	Sunderland	1997	34164
44	Birmingham City	2008	34286
45	Middlesbrough	1993	34340
46	Charlton Athletic	2007	34353
47	Bolton Wanderers	2012	34504
48	Birmingham City	2006	34861
49	Sheffield United	1994	34952
50	Crystal Palace	2005	35854
51	Sheffield United	2007	35977
52	Crystal Palace	1998	36722
	Watford	2018	37566
53	Fulham	2014	37669
54	Crystal Palace	1995	38738
55	Wimbledon	2000	39100
56	Portsmouth	2010	39413
57	Crystal Palace	1993	40342
58	Charlton Athletic	1999	41515
59	Watford	2007	42861
60	Bolton Wanderers	1998	44869
	Burnley	2018	45330
61	Bolton Wanderers	1996	45685
62	Watford	2000	46065
	Swansea City	2018	47293
63	Burnley	2015	47837
64	Hull City	2017	48004
65	Oldham Athletic	1994	48152
66	Reading	2013	48345
67	Wigan Athletic	2013	49298
68	Burnley	2010	49696
69	Hull City	2015	49851
70	Barnsley	1998	50724
71	Cardiff City	2014	50969
	Brighton & Hove Albion	2018	51035

72	Reading	2008	53632
73	Hull City	2010	54466
74	Swindon Town	1994	55041
	Huddersfield Town	2018	55364
75	Bradford City	2001	55929
	AFC Bournemouth	2018	56370
76	Blackpool	2011	57308

- It would be interesting to try and incorporate the number of trophies won by a team into the analysis, perhaps by deducting points – though deciding on the specifics of all this would introduce a hugely subjective factor. Is the Europa League worth more than the F.A. Cup? Does being the runner-up in the Champions League warrant anything? Likewise, adding a "fan-base" factor (using average attendances maybe?) would also be a nice addition, but again, brings considerable subjectivity.

- Whether or not the weighting of each year (e.g. season prior to relegation is worth 50, and then 49, 48, etc.) is appropriate is open to debate. In this analysis the weighting is linear, but it could be argued that this shouldn't be the case. Again though, deciding upon the weighting using a non-linear method would introduce far more subjectivity than using a simple, linear method.

- As explained at the start, the choice to use data from the previous 46 seasons was made because that was as far back as it was possible to go whilst keeping the sample sizes equal amongst all teams. Whilst (in my opinion) this was the best option to use, it could be argued that some teams are unfairly penalised in the analysis. For example, 55 years ago Burnley won the first division, and then followed that up with finishes of 4th, 2nd, and 3rd. Extending the data as far back as this would have made Burnley a "bigger club". That said, the weighting system used does mean these years aren't given as much influence, and so it is unlikely to have changed the table too much.

- Assigning an unconditional score of 50 points for all finishes outside of the top two tiers of English football could also be questioned. This decision was made because until 1959, the third division was split into North and South leagues, and therefore any finishes in these leagues would lead to ambiguity over an appropriate score to use. Whilst it is unlikely to have affected the top of the table (Villa dropped into the 3rd tier for only 2 seasons, whilst Leeds did not at all), it could be argued that this decision benefits some teams over others further down. For instance, 36 years before being relegated from the Premier League, Wimbledon were playing in the Isthmian Division – the 7th tier of English football. Assigning separate scores all the way down to this level would certainly have affected the results in this case.

ii.   Value for Money

- The age of players is taken from the time of the transfer (according to www.transfermarkt.com).
- The subjective decision to use a figure of 15% to deduct from the transfer fee in the *cost per season* formula for English players could – as stated in 'The Line Ups' – be debated. Out of interest, changing this figure to 10%

moves Sterling up one place to 11th most expensive player (now £3.98m per season), and moves Stones up two places to joint 13th most expensive (now £3.54m per season). Changing this figure to 20% moves Sterling down two places to joint 13th most expensive player (now £3.54m per season), and moves Stones down two places to 17th most expensive player (now £3.15m per season).

- Anthony Martial's transfer fee has since risen due to clauses in the initial deal. It is now stated to be £51.00 million.

iii.   Grinding out a Result

- Not all one-goal margin victories are necessarily "a grind". For example, in September 2016 Tottenham Hotspur beat Sunderland 1-0 in the Premier League. They had 31 shots compared to Sunderland's 6, and had 64% possession. By contrast, teams may win by two or even three in much more closely fought matches that are likely perceived as more of a "grind" by the players and managers. Late goals that occur as a team becomes more attacking in search of an equaliser may also obscure the true reflection of a match. Indeed, in the same month that Tottenham narrowly beat Sunderland despite dominating them throughout, Arsenal scored 83rd and 91st minute goals to change a seemingly tight 2-1 victory over Hull City into an apparently comfortable 4-1 victory. Whilst these examples are valid caveats, accounting for all of these detailed elements would be very difficult.

iv.   The Most Competitive League in the World

- The argument that larger TV revenues are indicative of a more competitive league is up for debate. It could be reasoned that such figures are a response to the imbalanced favouritism towards the top clubs in the league – with the smaller clubs (i.e., AFC Bournemouth, Watford, Burnley, etc.) benefitting from the global attention and support given to a few (i.e., Manchester United, Arsenal, Chelsea, etc.). However, based on this logic, similar revenues should stream into Spain's La Liga, where Real Madrid and Barcelona have arguably as big (or even greater) global appeal than any English club, yet this does not occur.

- Average points earned per game is used rather than simple point's totals because it allows the analysis to account for differences in the number of teams in a league, and therefore the varying number of matches played. The German Bundesliga, for example, is an 18-team, 34-game league, whereas the other four leagues are all 20-team, 38-game leagues. Notably the other four leagues have also all varied their numbers over the 23 season time-span of this analysis.

- Prior to the 1995/96 season in Spain and Germany, and the 1994/95 season in Italy and France, 2 points were awarded for a win, rather than the current 3 points. For the sake of these analyses, the values have been adjusted so that a win receives 3 points. In some cases this may mean a team should have finished higher in the league (for example, Barcelona in the 1994/95 La Liga season), though for this analysis the original league positions were kept the same.

- In the 2005/06 season in Italy, the Calciopoli scandal resulted in numerous teams being retrospectively docked points and consequently many league position changes occurred. As these were substantial *retrospective* punishments, it was decided that the pre-scandal points and positions would be used in the analyses. The same is true for the league positions from the 1992-93 French Ligue 1 season following the Olympique Marseille bribery scandal. In other situations where the points deduction occurred during the season (e.g. Portsmouth in 2009/10 and Parma in 2014/15), it was again decided to use the values such that no deductions had taken place. This is because it was felt the competitiveness of the team – which is what is being analysed – would be unfairly skewed otherwise.

- As explained in 'The Line Ups' section, comparing the top and bottom 4 teams was deemed most appropriate. However, it could be reasoned that – based on the logic used – a greater number than this should be included. Indeed, a 5 v 5 analysis might favour the Premier League given its historical media narrative of there being a "big four" group of teams. Yet expanding the analysis even further would result in 50% (or more) of a league being included, which defies the original intentions of the argument of comparing the top teams and the bottom teams.

- Data for the first method ('Points Spread') was collected from the last 25 seasons (1992/93 to 2016/17). Data for the second method ('Winning Margins') was collected from the last 6 seasons (2011/12 to 2016/17).

- The Bundesliga only contains 18 teams so in the 'Winning Margins' analysis, data is extrapolated to account for 20 teams like the other leagues. Interestingly, even without extrapolating the data to account for the fewer teams, the Bundesliga would still have recorded the second most number of 4+ victory margins over the past 5 seasons, with 109 instances in total.

v.   Why Rooney Should Blame Ronaldo

- As with a number of these chapters, in order to keep the analysis manageable, the myriad of other factors that determine ability are not considered. In this case, we only look at goal-scoring. This, however, is what defines a forward, and therefore seems an appropriate measure. Nevertheless, other contributions, be it assists, chances created, general passing, defensive attributes, and leadership are also important for a footballer, and it could be argued that this should be taken into account when comparing the likes of Rooney, Ronaldo, Tevez, Torres, and Drogba. It is questionable whether analysing such data (if it even exists) would shed any further light on why Rooney receives so much criticism, given that many of these are areas of his game that are often considered strengths.

- The data for goals scored by Ronaldo, Tevez, Torres, and Drogba includes that from leagues other than the Premier League, making direct comparisons with Wayne Rooney's total not completely fair. Indeed, a portion of Tevez and Drogba's goals are taken from considerably less renowned leagues such as the Chinese Super League, Turkish Super Lig, and Argentine Primera Division. Whilst it could be argued that it is easier to score in these leagues, an equal case could be put forward that with lesser-talented teammates (with no disrespect to these teams/players) the opportunities to score may also be fewer and harder. As such, the data regarding these goals may not be unfairly affected, though it is still an important point to acknowledge.

vi.   Europe: In or Out?

- The data showing that teams which remain in Europe tend to decrease their league points by 1.0 is based on 80 instances recorded using essentially the same method as described in 'The Line Ups'. The only exception being that these instances were of teams who remained in Europe for consecutive seasons (*in to in*). For instance, each of Arsenal's seasons from 2000/01 have involved European competition, therefore each change in points total between seasons would constitute an *in to in* instance.

vii.   The Big 6-Pointer

- A limitation in the data collection method used is that the selection of teams is a retrospective one. That is, the points the RS teams earned against a team are then related to that team's final league position – not the position they were in prior to the match against the RS team. Therefore what may at the time have been a match against a TC (or MT or RS) team may not be by the end of the season.

viii.   The Kante Effect

- As with the 'Extraordinary Managers' analysis, the data values refer to the effects on a team's league performance in terms of points accrued. As such, cup competitions are ignored. Clearly this is something to consider when opining about which players have truly influenced their new club the most, along with other factors such as impact on finances and attendances (like

David Beckham at L.A. Galaxy), or alterations in a club's style of play (such as Dennis Bergkamp at Arsenal).

- Only seasons in which a player played in at least 50% of the club's games are eligible for analysis. This is done to ensure that they do actually have an 'impact', and eliminates instances where a) a player transferred during the middle of the season, b) a player incurs a long-term injury, c) an older player gradually becomes less involved in a club before leaving, and d) any other such scenarios that may negatively skew the results.

- Like in the 'Extraordinary Managers' analysis data can only be compared within the same division, and as such, any instances in which the team that a player arrives at or leaves from has changed divisions are not included. For instance, when Nicolas Anelka arrived at Manchester City they had just been promoted to the Premier League. Comparing the pre-arrival league points (99 in the First Division) with the first season league points (51 in the Premier League) would not produce fair results.

- There is one instance in which the data is extrapolated. This is Zlatan Ibrahimovic's first season at Juventus. Here Serie A changed from a 34 game season to a 38 game season, and therefore to ensure a fair comparison with the 'pre' score, an extrapolated value was necessary.

- Given the subjective nature of the sample chosen, I am happy – in fact, 'eager' might be a better word! – to produce a follow up analysis with suggestions of other players. Feel free to contact me via the details given in the 'Postface'.

ix.   The Value of a Cup Run

- Statements in 'The Warm Up' regarding rested players by Everton, West Bromwich Albion, AFC Bournemouth, and Stoke City are based on the number of players in the starting 11 of each team's F.A. Cup third round match that, by the end of the season, had started less than 50% of the club's league matches.

x.   The League of Extraordinary Managers

- Only full seasons are taken into account. This means that instances such as Mourinho's tumultuous end at Chelsea (second time around), in which the Premier League champions had just 15 points from 16 games before dismissing the manager, are not used in the analysis. It would be possible to include such examples by extrapolating the data such that it represents a full season, but doing so would introduce other factors that may skew the results to an even greater degree. For example, the issue of regression to the mean (the natural return of an extreme value to its norm) has been well documented with regards manager in's and out's[4], and thus, taking data from mid-points of a season would likely exacerbate this problem further. The reverse of this is also true: Jurgen Klopp took over Liverpool *during* the 2015/16 Premier League season, meaning that this season neither counts towards his first full season, or the full season before for comparison.
- The warm-up states that the average league points earned each season by a manager is compared with that of the season before his arrival and after his departure. This isn't actually quite true. Rather, it is the

points earned per game that is compared. This is to account for any leagues in which the number of games in a season differs (e.g. the German Bundesliga).

- Sample sizes (i.e. number of clubs managed from which data is eligible) are small and uneven. This is an unescapable scenario, but it is still important to note when analysing the data.

	Sample Size Impact on Arrival	Sample Size Impact on Departure
Antonio Conte	3	1
Pep Guardiola	3	2
Jurgen Klopp	3	2
Jose Mourinho	6	5
Mauricio Pochettino	2	2
Arsene Wenger	3	1

- Managers of clubs "yo-yo-ing" between divisions further complicates the analyses as data can only be compared across the same division. For example, Southampton achieving 88 points in the Championship prior to Pochettino's arrival cannot be compared with the 56 points achieved in the Premier League in Pochettino's first full season. The same is true for managerial departures (Arsene Wenger left Nancy at the end of the season in which they were relegated). This again means such data cannot be included, and again, decreases the sample size.
- Another confounding factor is that managers are likely to be hired on the back of a team underperforming, and therefore improvements in performance should be expected. Guardiola's arrival at Barcelona and Conte's arrival at Juventus are good examples of this. This

should not completely detract from their achievements though, as Louis Van Gaal's tenure at Manchester United shows that it is still not easy to follow up what was a "poor campaign" by the predecessor. It is, however, worth noting, especially when a manager like Jose Mourinho has been unique and done the opposite – often arriving on the back of a very good season for the club. This relates back to the idea of regression to the mean discussed in chapter 6 'Europe: In or Out'.

- It could also be argued that the data used for the pre-arrival and post-departure values should be based on more than just one season. Taking an average of, say, three seasons prior to a managers arrival may provide a more accurate reflection of the club's true level and reduce the effects of any potential regression to the mean. However, the availability of such data is limited (see caveat number 4 above), and in any case, the method is the same for all managers so the like-for-like comparisons should not be biased in one particular way.

- As stated in the Warm-Up, it is important to acknowledge other factors that contribute to how highly a manager is rated. However, like in the 'Too Big To Go Down' analysis (chapter 1), trying to incorporate subjective aspects – such as playing style and personality – would prove very problematic. Even trying to account for more objective measures such as trophies won and money spent would introduce numerous difficulties given the variations in such factors across time and league (E.g. Is winning the F.A. Cup a greater achievement than winning the Coppa Italia? Should spending £10 million on players in 2005 be regarded as the same as spending £100 on players in 2015?)

xi.   He's Come Back to Haunt Them

- The key for Graph 1. is shown below.

		Ratio Difference
1	Emile Heskey vs Leicester City	0.22
2	Andrew Cole vs Newcastle United	0.10
3	Nicolas Anelka vs Bolton Wanderers	0.09
4	Peter Crouch vs Portsmouth	0.09
5	Peter Crouch vs Southampton	0.09
6	Alan Shearer vs Blackburn Rovers	0.08
7	Dion Dublin vs Coventry City	0.08
8	Peter Crouch vs Aston Villa	0.05
9	Frank Lampard vs West Ham United	0.03
10	Nicolas Anelka vs Arsenal	0.03
11	Darren Bent vs Tottenham Hotspur	0.02
12	Jermain Defoe vs West Ham United	0.01
13	Robin van Persie vs Arsenal	-0.01
14	Nicolas Anelka vs Manchester City	-0.04
15	Les Ferdinand vs Newcastle United	-0.06
16	Teddy Sheringham vs Nottingham Forest	-0.08
17	Peter Crouch vs Liverpool	-0.09
18	Nicolas Anelka vs Liverpool	-0.10
19	Dwight Yorke vs Aston Villa	-0.13
20	Jermain Defoe vs Tottenham Hotspur	-0.17
21	Wayne Rooney vs Everton	-0.18
22	Teddy Sheringham vs Tottenham Hotspur	-0.18
23	Emile Heskey vs Liverpool	-0.21
24	Emile Heskey vs Birmingham City	-0.21
25	Emile Heskey vs Wigan Athletic	-0.21
26	Peter Crouch vs Tottenham Hotspur	-0.24
27	Jimmy Floyd Hasselbaink vs Chelsea	-0.27
28	Robbie Fowler vs Liverpool	-0.29
29	Dion Dublin vs Manchester United	-0.31
30	Dwight Yorke vs Manchester United	-0.33

31	Dwight Yorke vs Blackburn Rovers	-0.33
32	Teddy Sheringham vs Manchester United	-0.35
33	Andrew Cole vs Manchester United	-0.37
34	Jimmy Floyd Hasselbaink vs Leeds United	-0.44
35	Michael Owen vs Liverpool	-0.46

- All data is taken from soccerbase.com and is based on league goals only. Appearances include those made from the substitute's bench. Analysing minutes per goal, rather than goals per game, would provide a fairer reflection of goal-scoring ability and tendency to "come back to haunt" a team, however, this data is largely inaccessible, inconsistent, or unreliable, particularly for older players.

- Jermain Defoe has since left Sunderland and joined AFC Bournemouth. However, until he returns to play the Black Cats 5 times this will not have any impact on the data collected or the results found. Given the respective divisions of the two clubs and Defoe's age, it is unlikely that these 5 matches will ever occur.

14. References

i.   Too Big To Go Down

1) For transfer spending of Arsenal, Tottenham Hotspur, Manchester City, Manchester United, and Chelsea during the 2015/16 season:
http://www.transfermarkt.co.uk/premier-league/sommertransfers/wettbewerb/GB1/plus/?saison_id=2015&s_w=&leihe=0&leihe=1&intern=0&intern=1

2) All main data (i.e. the season by season positions of relegated clubs, notable cases, and 2018 Premier League teams) is taken from www.statto.com

ii.   Value for Money

1) The Telegraph's statement regarding Raheem Sterling's transfer to Manchester City:
http://www.telegraph.co.uk/sport/football/teams/manchester-city/11736078/Raheem-Sterling-Why-have-Manchester-City-paid-49m-for-him.html

2) The Telegraph's statement regarding John Stones' transfer to Manchester City:
http://www.telegraph.co.uk/football/2016/08/09/paul-pogba-price-isnt-particularly-crazy-the-transfer-market-wil/

3) The Mail Online's statement regarding EU eligibility requirements "pushing up transfer fees for those (English) types of players":
http://www.dailymail.co.uk/sport/article-3162269/Raheem-Sterling-s-Manchester-City-opened-discussion-Premier-League-s-homegrown-quota-does-actually-work.html

4) Premier League starting 11's from the 2015/16 season analysed to calculate the average age of each position are taken from www.whoscored.com

5) All transfer values are taken from www.transfermarkt.co.uk

iii.   Grinding out a Result

1) Jose Mourinho's penchant for grinding out a result:
https://www.thesun.co.uk/sport/football/2607245/jose-mourinho-manager-of-the-month-alex-ferguson-arsene-wenger-joe-kinnear/

2) Sir Alex Ferguson's quote that grinding out a result is part of the DNA that makes up champions: Worrall, F. (2014). Fergie: The Greatest – The Biography of Sir Alex Ferguson. London, England: John Blake Publishing.

3) Previous pseudo-analyses only taking into accounting 1-0 victories:
http://www.bbc.co.uk/sport/football/35969632

4) The most common victory in the English Premier League is 1-0 or 2-1: Anderson, C., & Sally, D. (2013). The Numbers Game. London, England: Penguin Books, Ltd.

5) Explanation of the narrative fallacy: Taleb, N.N. (2007). The Black Swan: The impact of the highly improbable. London, England: Penguin Books.

6) All data taken from www.statto.com

iv.   The Most Competitive League in the World

1) Opening quote regarding the use of clichés:
http://news.sky.com/story/ukraine-russia-bites-the-hand-that-feeds-10405842

2) The Premier League receives substantially greater television revenues than other world football leagues:
http://www.bbc.co.uk/news/business-22766638

3) The commonly held belief that the English Premier League, Spanish La Liga, German Bundesliga, Italian Serie A, and French Ligue 1 are the five best leagues in world football:
http://www2.deloitte.com/content/dam/Deloitte/uk/Documents/sports-business-group/deloitte-uk-annual-review-of-football-finance-2016.pdf

4) All data taken from the following three sources:
www.espn.co.uk/0/football, www.statto.com/football/teams, and www.worldfootball.net

v.   Why Rooney Should Blame Ronaldo

1) Jermain Defoe's reported £65,000 per week contract with AFC Bournemouth:
https://www.thesun.co.uk/sport/football/3629405/jermain-defoe-bournemouth-deal-65000-sunderland/

2) The unfair criticism that Wayne Rooney receives:
http://www.dailymail.co.uk/sport/football/article-

4525922/Man-United-s-Wayne-Rooney-doesn-t-credit-deserves.html

3) Wayne Rooney not living up to his potential: http://www.soccerbox.com/blog/wayne-rooney-ever-reach-full-potential/

4) The Guardian's article comparing Wayne Rooney with Pele: https://www.theguardian.com/uk/2004/jun/23/euro2004.football

5) All data taken from www.transfermarkt.com

vi.　　Europe: In or Out?

1) Chelsea, Liverpool, and Leicester benefitting from not having to play European football: https://www.theguardian.com/football/who-scored-blog/2016/nov/29/chelsea-liverpool-premier-league-champions

2) Reasons why a lack of European football may be beneficial to league performance: http://www.skysports.com/football/news/11096/10760144/have-chelsea-benefited-from-champions-league-and-europa-league-qualification-failure

3) Manchester City injuries in 2015/16: https://www.jlt.com/media-centre/news-and-press-releases/2016/august/injuries-cost-premier-league-clubs-157million

4) Manchester United injuries in 2016/17: http://www.physioroom.com/info/english-premier-league-injury-analysis-201617-season/

5) An explanation of egression to the mean:
https://en.wikipedia.org/wiki/Regression_toward_the_mean

6) All data was collected from www.statto.com

vii.   The Big 6-Pointer

1) Defining the cliché, "A Big 6-Pointer":
https://www.thesun.co.uk/sport/2232754/why-is-a-football-match-sometimes-described-as-a-six-pointer/

2) Mick McCarthy's decision to rest players in Wolverhampton Wanderers' match against Manchester United:
https://www.theguardian.com/football/2009/dec/16/mick-mccarthy-wolves-manchester-united

3) All data was collected from www.statto.com

viii.   The Kante Effect

1) Regarding articles praising Kante's statistical contributions in the Premier League:
http://www.standard.co.uk/sport/football/ngolo-kante-stats-show-why-chelsea-star-is-set-to-become-double-premier-league-title-winner-a3488756.html

2) References to transfers in 'The Warm Up' and all main data (i.e. transfer values) are taken from www.transfermarkt.co.uk

ix.   The Value of a Cup Run

1) Data regarding the starting XI's of Everton, Stoke City, West Bromwich Albion, and AFC Bournemouth was obtained from www.whoscored.com
2) Main data collected from www.statto.com

x.   The League of Extraordinary Managers

1) Mauricio Pochettino linked with the managerial job at Barcelona: http://www.dailymail.co.uk/sport/football/article-4503252/Pochettino-promises-lead-Tottenham-new-stadium.html
2) Mauricio Pochettino linked with the managerial job at Manchester United: http://www.telegraph.co.uk/sport/football/teams/manchester-united/12091554/Man-Utd-transfer-news-and-rumours-Mauricio-Pochettino-lined-up-as-Louis-van-Gaal-replacement.html
3) Data was collected from two sources: www.transfermarkt.com and www.statto.com
4) Anderson, C., & Sally, D. (2014). The Numbers Game: Why everything you know about football is wrong. London, England; Penguin Books.

xi.   He's Come Back to Haunt Them

1) Daily Mail headline after Frank Lampard scored Manchester City's equalising goal against his former

club Chelsea:
http://www.dailymail.co.uk/sport/football/article-2764331/Frank-Lampard-close-tears-lost-words-scoring-equaliser-didn-t-expect-Manchester-City-against-Chelsea.html.

2) Amos Tversky and Daniel Kahneman's seminal paper on the availability heuristic (Tversky, A., & Kahneman, D. (1973). Availability: A heuristic for judging frequency and probability. *Cognitive Psychology, 5*(2), 207-232): http://www.sciencedirect.com/science/article/pii/0010028573900339

3) A review of confirmation bias (Nickerson, R.S. (1998). Confirmation bias: A ubiquitous phenomenon in many guises. *Review of General Psychology, 2*(2), 175-220): http://psycnet.apa.org/index.cfm?fa=search.displayrecord&uid=1998-02489-003

4) Data for the analyses was taken from www.soccerbase.com

15. Postface

So there it is. Aston Villa. Because you need to take into account age and nationality. No. No. Because until 2010 they were very similar...then Cristiano Ronaldo became a freak of nature. Out. Yes. No...well, maybe Zlatan Ibrahimovic. No. Antonio Conte. And not as often as we're led to believe!

As mentioned on numerous occasions, these analyses are not rigorous, scientific evaluations of important and meaningful issues within football today. They are simply my way of providing a data-driven perspective on topics that I, and hopefully you the reader, find interesting. All data was painstakingly collected myself via various internet sources. They have been double and triple checked, though I would never want to make the guarantee that these analyses are completely error-free. As such, all data can be provided on request for anyone who wishes to check themselves, expand with their own, new data, or just take a closer look at the nitty gritty details.

Likewise, if you would like to propose any ideas for me to explore in the future I welcome all suggestions – no matter how far-fetched and impossible they may seem! The dream was to write a book, and I have now done that. If I am lucky enough to write a follow up to this then perhaps your idea will form one of these chapters. If not, then it may still turn up on a blog that I write for; the web address for this is listed below, along with my email address and twitter handle.

On the same lines, I would strongly encourage all forms of feedback – no matter how negative or critical it may be! If you believe something is wrong, think something could have been done better, or just want to tell me that you've wasted your money and it was a load of rubbish, please do! I'd rather know this than be unaware. And it may also have a cathartic benefit for you too!

Finally, I would like to say a massive thank you. Hopefully you have read the whole of the book and found it informative, interesting, and intelligently written, but even if you've just happened upon this page as it lay torn out on the floor next to a bin, I am grateful regardless.

I'll end this with a quote that sums up my feelings on completing this book, which has been four years in the making:

"I couldn't be more chuffed if I were a badger at the start of mating season"

Queens Park Rangers manager Ian Holloway after beating Cardiff City

Theinnergeekinfootball@gmail.com

Twitter: @the_innergeek

https://blog.playtogga.com/

20143066R00075

Printed in Poland
by Amazon Fulfillment
Poland Sp. z o.o., Wrocław